Successor journal to *Theatre Quarterly* (1971–1981)
VOLUME XVII   PART 4   (NTQ 68)
NOVEMBER 2001

Published in association with Rose Bruford College

D1743823

Editors
CLIVE BARKER
SIMON TRUSSLER

Associate Editor: Maggie Gale

Advisory Editors: Arthur Ballet, Eugenio Barba, Susan Bassnett, Tracy Davis, Martin Esslin, Lizbeth Goodman, Peter Hepple, Ian Herbert, Jan Kott, Bella Merlin (*Book Review Editor*), Brian Murphy, Maria Shevtsova, Sarah Stanton, Juliusz Tyszka, Ian Watson

Contents

New Theatre Quarterly is published in February, May, August, and November by Cambridge University Press, The Edinburgh Building, Shaftesbury Road, Cambridge CB2 2RU, England   ISBN 0 521 00284 2   ISSN 0266–464X

Editorial Enquiries

Oldstairs, Kingsdown, Deal, Kent CT14 8ES, England (e-mail: simontrussler@lineone.net)

Unsolicited manuscripts are considered for publication in *New Theatre Quarterly*. They may be sent to Simon Trussler either at the postal address above or as e-mail attachments. Intending contributors should follow the journal's house style as closely as possible. A style sheet is available on request, or may be downloaded from the journal's website.

Subscriptions

New Theatre Quarterly (ISSN: 0266-464X) is published quarterly by Cambridge University Press, The Edinburgh Building, Shaftesbury Road, Cambridge CB2 2RU, UK, and The Journals Department, 40 West 20th Street, New York, NY 10011-4211, USA.

Four parts form a volume. The subscription price, which includes postage (excluding VAT), of Volume XVII, 2001, is £58.00 (US$95.00 in the USA, Canada and Mexico) for institutions, £32.00 (US$50.00) for individuals ordering direct from the publishers and certifying that the Journal is for their personal use. Single parts cost £16.00 (US$26.00 in the USA, Canada and Mexico) plus postage. EU subscribers (outside the UK) who are not registered for VAT should add VAT at their country's rate. VAT registered subscribers should provide their VAT registration number. Prices include delivery by air. Japanese prices for institutions are available from Kinokuniya Company Ltd., P.O. Box 55, Chitose, Tokyo 156, Japan.

Orders, which must be accompanied by payment, may be sent to a bookseller or to the publishers (in the USA, Canada and Mexico to the North American Branch). Periodicals postage paid at New York, NY, and at additional mailing offices. POSTMASTER: send address changes in the USA, Canada and Mexico to *New Theatre Quarterly*, Cambridge University Press, The Journals Fulfillment Department, 110 Midland Avenue, Port Chester, NY 10573-4930.

Claims for missing issues will only be considered if made immediately on receipt of the following issue.

Information on *New Theatre Quarterly* and all other Cambridge journals can be accessed via http://www.cambridge.org/.

© 2001 CAMBRIDGE UNIVERSITY PRESS

The Edinburgh Building, Cambridge CB2 2RU, United Kingdom
40 West 20th Street, New York, NY 10011-4211, USA
10 Stamford Road, Oakleigh, Melbourne 3166, Australia
Ruiz de Alarcón 13, 28014 Madrid, Spain

Typeset by Country Setting, Kingsdown, Deal, Kent CT14 8ES
Printed and bound in the United Kingdom at the University Press, Cambridge

Jim Davis and Victor Emeljanow

'Wistful Remembrancer': the Historiographical Problem of Macqueen-Popery

The theatre shelves of secondhand bookshops testify to the sometime popularity and prolific output of the theatre publicist and would-be historian Walter Macqueen-Pope. Yet even by the time Macqueen-Pope was publishing his later volumes in the 1950s, the rise of academic theatre scholarship was questioning such anecdotally based and unverified accounts of the theatre and its past. Today, we can look at Macqueen-Pope, and at the period immediately before the First World War which was so often the focus of his attention, not so much for evidence of flawed scholarship as for his revealing attitude towards his subject and its social context. For anecdotage and nostalgia have inevitably to be taken into account in any historical approach to so ephemeral an art as the theatre, and, as the authors here conclude, while Macqueen-Pope may not tell us the whole truth about his many subjects, such a 'wistful remembrancer' remains significant to any investigation of a theatrical past 'that must always be a melting pot of imperfect recognitions and unattainable desires'. Jim Davis is Associate Professor of Theatre and Head of the School of Theatre, Film and Dance at the University of New South Wales. Victor Emeljanow is Professor of Drama and Head of the Department of Drama at the University of Newcastle, New South Wales. Both have written extensively on nineteenth-century British theatre and are the joint authors of *Reflecting the Audience: London Theatregoing 1840–1880*, which has just been published by the University of Iowa Press.

An age which has Speed allied to Noise as its god cannot be expected to have long memories – can hardly remember contemporary happenings, let alone what happened yesterday or the day before.[1]

A man of middle age stood in the vestibule of the theatre. He – being of his period – was in evening dress. Before his startled eyes passed a cavalcade of five people – two women and three quite young children. None of them were in evening dress – they were not even in their best dresses. That would not have mattered. But the two women carried string bags full of vegetables and all five were licking ice-cream cornets. They passed into the stalls. They had paid sixteen and sixpence each. They were entitled to go into the stalls; they were entitled to carry string bags of vegetables – and presumably they were entitled to lick ice-cream cornets. Yet, somehow, it did not seem right to the middle-aged man. It seemed to him a portent. It seemed to him that the Theatre had fallen from the standard and dignity which it once held. There was a time when people thus

attired, thus laden, and thus occupied, would not have been allowed to go into the stalls. And, if possessed of tickets, their money would have been returned and they would have – most politely – been shown the door.[2]

Memories are the preservative of youth. If you can remember, you can be young.[3]

RAPHAEL SAMUEL in *Theatres of Memory* draws on the metaphor of theatrical illusion to advocate the importance of popular memory as a factor in our engagement with the past and as a way of constructing knowledge:

Memory is not merely an image bank of the past but an active shaping force: that is, it is dynamic – what it contrives symptomatically to forget is as important as what it remembers.[4]

Popular memory, says Samuel, 'provides a sense of the past at any given point in time and is as much a matter of history as what

299

happened in it'.[5] In a way, popular memory has operated on both sides of the curtain in that it has also impacted on the reminiscences of theatre practitioners, playgoers, and critics. In English theatrical criticism, at least from the time of Charles Lamb and William Hazlitt, memory and nostalgia have played a significant role. To Hazlitt, writes T. N. Talfourd, 'The theatre was redolent of the past . . . imperfect recognitions of a hundred evenings, when mirth or sympathy had loosened the pressure at the heart, and set the springs of life in happier motion, thronged around him. . . . '[6] Charles Dickens has similar recollections, as in his invocation of the childhood pleasures of pantomime in his Introduction to the *Memoirs of Grimaldi*.[7] And, in some of the sources available for researching into late nineteenth- and early twentieth-century theatregoing, nostalgia and memory are also prominent.

This is especially the case in the work of Walter Macqueen-Pope, a critic who has long been dismissed on account of the occasional inaccuracies, opinionated diatribes, and seemingly irrelevant anecdotes that sometimes characterize his work: hence our notion of 'Macqueen-Popery'. Yet, as with the work of his contemporary, the critic A. E. Wilson, personal memories – 'imperfect recognitions' as defined by Talfourd – inform many of his accounts of the theatrical past. Indeed, imperfect recognition is the basis of many of the reviews, reminiscences, and surveys which provide part of the source material through which we investigate the theatrical past.

The Nature of Nostalgia

Such insubstantiality is part of the pleasure of historiography, but it is the complicating factor of nostalgia – in which memory and other concomitant associations often engage in a rewriting of the past – which we particularly want to consider, and specifically in relation to Macqueen-Pope. In doing so we are not necessarily problematizing nostalgia, but seeking to identify its possibilities for a rounded and representative investigation of the way in which the theatrical past is constituted.

There have been a number of studies of nostalgia, some based clearly in sociological or cognitive discourses, others ranging more broadly. Susan Stewart's focuses particularly on nostalgia associated with mementos and objects. The 'social disease of nostalgia',[8] as Stewart calls it, seems to involve the creation of an imagined or constructed past often related to a period when life seemed secure, unthreatening, and, significantly, unchanging. It is also of course related to particular periods in one's life, such as adolescence and childhood. Fred Davis suggests that nostalgia leaps backwards into the past to rediscover and revere it, and that it 'thrives on transition, on the subjective discontinuities that engender our yearning for continuity'.[9]

Macqueen-Pope seems oblivious to nostalgia when he discusses memories, which he calls 'about the greatest gift mankind was ever granted'.[10] In a passage which comes close to acknowledging his own tendencies as a writer, he claims:

So powerful are memories that every generation since the world began has always imagined – and quite rightly – that the days when it was young were the best days; that the things that happened then were so infinitely superior to what is happening now, that old friends, old customs, old songs, old plays and players were far and away better than the 'trash' which their juniors acclaim. Nothing today is ever quite so good. . . . The ideal form of existence is to be able to be aware of the present, but to live in the past.[11]

For Macqueen-Pope the capacity to recall the past is particularly important in dealing with theatre, since acting is the most ephemeral of all arts. 'All that the actor of yesterday could do', he says, 'was to leave a memory of his art in the memory of the people who saw him.'[12] In other words, it is through popular memory that the theatrical past may be retrieved, through one's own recollections as well as those of others.

One of Macqueen-Pope's fellow chroniclers and contemporaries of the Edwardian theatre, A. E. Wilson, is open not only about memory (and its unreliability), but also about his own nostalgia for the past:

I am old enough alas! to boast that I can remember what the world was like when the century

His Majesty's Theatre, from the Haymarket. Erected by Beerbohm Tree in 1896, this epitomized in terms of new theatre building what Macqueen-Pope felt to be the 'stable and secure' world its patrons inhabited.

began. One's childhood memories grow dim and no doubt they are coloured a good deal by nostalgic sentiment. But to me the impression remains of a pleasant, easy-going era. . . .[13]

For Macqueen-Pope, who could also remember as far back, the Edwardian era was memorable for its stability and slow pace:

Progress was going on all around, but nobody paid much attention to it. . . . England had not yet become Great Britain in our speech; we were still insular, still sure of ourselves with the deepest confidence. . . . The Empire was our God and Kipling was its prophet. . . . But the changes were coming leisurely in the good old British way, and we had no reason to suppose that the twentieth century would not be the same as the nineteenth.[14]

The theatre in this period, says Macqueen-Pope, was as 'stable and secure as the life of its patrons':

It was – far more than it is today [1947] – . . . a true microcosm of London. . . . It was conducted with a dignity and courtesy not understood at all today. It disregarded the outside march of progress and had nothing to do with rush or vulgar clamour.[15]

All this is written without irony and without any conscious acknowledgement of nostalgia. The world of the past is an uncomplicated place in which class and gender divisions are clearly both demarcated and reflected in the theatre, a theatre which represents stability and tradition. In the same year that saw the publication of his study of the Edwardian theatre, Macqueen-Pope's portrait of the Haymarket Theatre appeared. Enter this theatre, he declaims, and

Gone is the noise, the strident sounds of mechanism; gone the cosmopolitan mobs of the pavements, the modern misses in trousers and the modern men in pullovers and corduroys. . . . There is no braying of saxophones here, no jungle noises; this is a place for spinets and harp, for the delicate throb of the violin, for this is an English theatre keeping its English atmosphere in an English city which has lost too much of its native breath and custom.[16]

For Macqueen-Pope the English theatre was forever England and, whatever changes it had to weather in a turbulent present, it was also and inexorably the repository of a golden past.

Macqueen-Pope's sense of nostalgia almost anticipates Frederic Jameson's perception of the postmodern condition, in which a discomfort with contemporary existence leads to a desire to live in an eternal present based on an ahistoricized past. Hal Foster summarizes Jameson's argument as

the wish to be called to times less problematic than our own. This in turn points to a refusal to engage the present or to think historically – a refusal that Jameson regards as characteristic of the 'schizophrenia' of consumer society.[17]

The Failure to Think Historically

While Macqueen-Pope might posthumously object to any association, however spurious, with postmodernism (and indeed his nostalgia obviously lacks the complexities and ironies of postmodernist discourse), he surely would have felt at home with those writers and painters described by Anne C. Colley in her study *Nostalgia and Recollection in Victorian Culture*, who

at moments feel alienated from their homeland and their origins by virtue of distance, age, or alteration. All of them intermittently suffer from a desire for reunion, for some point of correspondence between their present and their past. . . . Caught in circumstances that dispossess and trap them in the tensions between the real and the remembered, these figures . . . write or paint toward home in an attempt to reach a place where there is a possibility of continuity and where there is a sanctuary from the changes that come with the passing of time. Often their texts offer them a form of hope, of promise, that they can, for a moment, place themselves in the track of their former selves and re-enter what is now irrevocably absent and seemingly unavailable. They can reclaim what was once themselves.[18]

This is not however merely an exercise in the recovery of self or of identity. Colley suggests that these writers and artists use nostalgia 'to sometimes fictionalize and sentimentalize a past that never fully existed', but that 'their longing often gives them the means to move beyond themselves and their past – it creates new maps'.[19] Yet, if 'new maps' are

being created, what function do they have in our investigation of the past?

When Macqueen-Pope died in 1960 at the age of 72 our understanding of popular theatregoing in the period to the Second World War, especially from 1897 to 1914, was predominantly influenced by a number of his books, which included *Carriages at Eleven* (1947), *Shirtfronts and Sables* (1953), and *Nights of Gladness* (1956). Yet, surprisingly, A. E. Wilson's *Edwardian Theatre*[20] does not refer to him at all, J. C. Trewin's *Edwardian Theatre* describes him as 'a wistful remembrancer',[21] and Allardyce Nicoll refers to his work only in passing.[22]

Yet here was a man who had written at least fifteen books, including histories of major theatres like Drury Lane, the Haymarket and the St. James's, a history of musical comedy, and an account of female performers on the English stage from 1660 down to the close of the Victorian period. Unlike his slightly older contemporary Wilson or his younger contemporary Trewin, he had not been a journalist or a critic for the London papers. He had been an 'insider', part of the business of purveying popular entertainment.

Macqueen-Pope's father abandoned his family and a sickly wife, who subsequently died in her thirties. Macqueen-Pope was largely brought up by an uncle and two maiden aunts, who introduced him to the theatre – he remembered them taking him to the first night of *The Belle of New York* for his tenth birthday in 1898. Thus *Carriages at Eleven* represents the memories of someone coming to popular entertainment at his most impressionable: he was just twelve when the Edwardian era commenced.

He spent a short period of employment as a shipping clerk, but at the age of twenty he received his first taste of the theatre business. He became the private secretary of George Dance, who then controlled most of the touring circuits and through whom he first met George Edwardes. At the onset of the First World War he became Alfred Butt's business manager, and in that capacity handled the business of the St. James's, Globe, the Palace of Varieties, Covent Garden, and the Lyric. He also became Charles Frohman's publicity

Walter Macqueen-Pope: the young man about town of 21, and the 'wistful remembrancer' half a century later.

officer, and after the war managed the Duke of York's, Whitehall, and Aldwych Theatres and Alexandra Palace. From 1918 he managed the publicity for Julian Wylie, Seymour Hicks, and H. M. Tennant's, and from 1935 appears to have been the spokesperson for most West End theatres till after the Second World War.

Looking Backwards

On the face of it, Macqueen-Pope was in an ideal position to be authoritative about the theatre practices he encountered from 1908, when he commenced his first theatrical employment. His associations brought him into intimate contact with the purveyors of popular entertainment – in particular pantomime, musical comedy, and revue – in both the West End and the provinces. Why then has his reputation been called into question?

Scholarly interest in Edwardian theatre is relatively new, and inevitably a point of departure has been Macqueen-Pope's 1947 study, *Carriages at Eleven*. Yet recent scholarship has drawn attention to the turmoil and insecurity of the period, in contradiction to

Macqueen-Pope's identification of it as an age of security and stability.[23] *Carriages at Eleven* privileges the class of theatregoers who could afford just such vehicles while ignoring those who could not, and evokes an era of leisurely pursuits and behaviour at odds with mechanical progress. But such progress was already in train: the official speed limit on cars had been lifted to twenty mph in 1903, and the bioscope was a regular feature on music-hall bills.

Just as detrimental to Macqueen-Pope's posthumous reputation has been his dismissal of many progressive developments in the late nineteenth and early twentieth centuries, such as the suffrage movement and the embryonic welfarFe state – as well as his uncritical support of actor-managers, whose urbanity, expertise, and sheer maleness he admired. Much of Macqueen-Pope's work is thus a celebration of the heyday of the actor-manager, with its dependence on individualism and free enterprise.

While his subsequent histories of theatres with which he had had dealings through Dance, Edwardes, Butt, or Hicks have often been regarded as unscholarly and anecdotal,

The dress code that disappeared: illustration from *Ghosts and Greasepaint* of stalls patrons in the Edwardian theatre.

standards.' Instituted in wartime, these continued into the period of post-war austerity after Attlee's Labour Party had resoundingly defeated Churchill's Conservatives in 1945. The book was thus written for posterity in a world of food rationing, of nationalization of the key industries of transport, coal, and steel, and of the inception of the National Health Service.

The Loss of Individualism

To Macqueen-Pope, this concept of social service built into the machinery of state was anathema. It signalled the end of individualism and, coupled with his abhorrence of mechanical mass entertainment, the end of an era. Given that all his books were written in this context, it is hardly surprising that they are suffused by a sense of personal loss. Over and over, he draws the attention of the reader to the names of actors who have recently died and notes with gratitude those old actors who are still alive. Many of his books reflect his own peregrinations round London, during which he constantly draws attention to those landmarks which have disappeared and to those which have survived. He consistently juxtaposes a present of dispiriting and indiscriminate sameness with a past which celebrated individuality.

And individualism was very important to Macqueen-Pope. 'W. Macqueen-Pope is the only bearer of that name in the world', states the biography printed on the dust jacket of *The Footlights Flickered*. In his advocacy of the free market, opposition to subsidy and the welfare state, and support for individualism he sounds like a prophet of Thatcherism – the policies of which he would doubtless have applauded, while deploring their vulgarity. The 'carriage folk' are celebrated for their unflagging retention of 'individualism', for the great store they set by 'quality', and for their refusal to follow the herd.

Music-hall performers were the 'supreme individualists of an individual age',[24] 'the very peak of Individualism', 'models of Individualism, private enterprise *in excelsis*'.[25] The old actors and actresses were also strong individualists: they had no desire to be other

these books still retain a value as documents that may contribute to historical analysis, even if they are unreliable as verifiable historical accounts in themselves. For through Macqueen-Pope's attitudes, prejudices, and memories, however much coloured by nostalgia, we see the emergence of a history we cannot ignore, even if we must simultaneously question its authenticity. It is a history seen from a particular perspective – ideologically different from today's, but one that has inevitably informed our own attitudes and prejudices, even if only in reaction to Macqueen-Pope's assumptions.

The title-page verso of *Carriages at Eleven* carries, following a cramped dedication to Macqueen-Pope's grandchildren, the statement that 'This book is produced in complete conformity with the authorized economy than as they were, and preserved their mystique through their limited public exposure outside of the theatre. But the world of the early 1950s was different. 'This is not an Individualistic age', lamented Macqueen-Pope wistfully, 'this is an age of One Class – we have been levelled.'[26]

Social Change, Disappearing Dress Codes

Macqueen-Pope is at his best when he moves in for a close-up to look at the achievements of such figures as Oswald Stoll, Matheson Lang, Marie Tempest, Gertie Millar, or, a little nearer to the time of his writing, Gracie Fields. He had an evident fascination for contrast and contradiction displayed by the individuals he admired. On a personal level, he forgave the less than glamorous elements of personal idiosyncrasy on the grounds of individual and enduring contributions to the practices of theatre. He thus had a predilection for those individuals who exhibited a combination of ruthlessness and urbanity, glamour and hard-headed business sense.

Yet even here he was selective: he devoted a considerable amount of space to George Dance, who gave him his first theatrical position, but virtually ignored C. B. Cochran, not only the most significant entrepreneur and showman of the period 1914–39, but also a man with whom he had dealings for a far longer period. Though Dance was transparently a manipulative ogre with 'eyes that were fiery – not bloodshot but literally fiery', he was also a successful writer of musical comedy, the licensee of most of the West End theatre bars, and his twenty-four touring companies took their gospel of West End theatre values into the provinces. Cochran in contrast was a vulgar showman, with 'a florid complexion, quiet voice and pale eyes which always hid his thoughts', who 'got the public to take him at his own valuation'. In Macqueen-Pope's view, the man 'who can thus impose himself on the masses must be a genius'.[27]

It is when he steps back to place those achievements within their contexts that Macqueen-Pope's prejudices and limitations become apparent. The past becomes a world

The end of Macqueen-Pope's world: the great theatrical restaurant closed – and renamed as an American bar.

in which one 'lived in a land that was law abiding and where crime was almost negligible, where the standard of living for all classes was the highest in the world, where money went far and the proportion of paupers was very small'.[28] There is of course considerable naivety in this point of view, and this is reflected equally in his view of the early nineteenth century:

Drunkenness was the curse of the time, chiefly because there was little else for the lower classes to do but drink. . . . Yet . . . there was nothing like the amount of crime that there is in this year of grace 1950. Crime was then a purely professional affair and not very profitable.[29]

As far as Macqueen-Pope was concerned, respectable citizens were now deterred from visiting the theatre for fear of burglary while they left their homes unoccupied. His resistance to progress, social equality, technology (such as the car, the cinema, and television) is also a reaction to the destabilizing impact of the First and Second World Wars:

The First World War was of course a social revolution. Men were snatched from every rank of life and thrust into uniform; they all went into the melting pot and were shaken up together. Women who had lived domestic and secluded lives went out into commerce and factories doing men's jobs. Wise people foretold that good would come of this – a better understanding between the various strata of what then composed society. But that did not come about.[30]

In the good old days prior to the First World War, the working class knew its place:

It worked hard, it worked long hours. . . . It was proud of its country, it was proud to be British. . . . It believed that as a race it was superior to all the rest of the world. It pitied and even despised foreigners. . . . It wallowed in sentimentality, and it cheered the Union Jack. It was a proud race . . . with a tremendous loyalty to the throne and a respect for those of high rank which, in its unenlightened way, it still regarded as its 'betters'.[31]

Socialists, conspicuous in their red ties, were then 'unsuccessful shabby, hungry men who, disappointed in wealth and possessions themselves, had the idea of confiscating those estimable things which their more fortunate or more clever fellow-citizens had managed to secure'.[32] Economic decline and loss of empire are no less mourned, as is the constant decline in the quality of entertainment and of theatre audiences

Macqueen-Pope's disquiet with a changing world is also reflected in his comments on dress codes, both within the theatre and in society at large. *Shirtfronts and Sables* is partially a lament for the days when the socially diverse zones of the theatre auditorium required appropriate modes of dress and behaviour. Writing in 1953, he can hardly contain his outrage at the relaxation of the old conventions:

Quite recently the author and his wife attended a first night at the opera – and so they, in their innocence, put on their best evening clothes, he his stiff shirt, his stiff collar, his white tie, and tails. Except for the conductor, they were the only people so dressed. Just a few seats along the row, a couple had their supper out of a paper bag. Well, why not? That is the world of today.[33]

And contemporary fashions provoked similar reactions, especially if American. So women who wore trousers or who smoked earned his disapproval, as did jeans, bare feet, and pony tails. In the past, women had been 'essentially feminine. They wore low-cut gowns but they never made a display of their busts which is so apparent in girls today . . . they kept their legs a secret . . . '.[34] Modern girls, especially American ones, were only distinguishable from their male companions because of their 'high heels in wedge-like formation', 'masses of brassy, ill-dyed hair', and 'busts which protruded like the noses of submarines'.[35]

Even the West End prostitutes in Leicester Square no longer measured up. Once:

They had carriage and poise – they moved like mannequins for indeed they had something for sale. . . . But these women . . . were subjected to disgraceful semi-professional competition during World War Two by hordes of terrible teen-age girls of repellent habits and appearance, who infested the West End in particular, coming from heaven – or hell – knows where and eventually returning to the Stygian depths from which the war had called them . . . It was a shocking spectacle to which the First World War has no parallel.[36]

On stage too the decorum of the performers, clothed or unclothed, had been much greater in past times. Reflecting on stage nudity, Macqueen-Pope recalls how the Seldoms, once a popular music-hall act, had 'managed to combine a great deal of nudity with considerably more art than the nudes of today achieve'.[37]

Turning Back the Tide

Although Macqueen-Pope remains consistent throughout his writings, the ouput after *Carriages at Eleven* becomes more sombre. The exception is *The Melodies Linger On*, perhaps because in 1950 music hall and variety still appeared to have a life, even on television, which he normally despised. Many of the old stars were still alive and in any case the songs were still current. *Nights of Gladness*, however, chronicles the demise of native musical comedy in the face of revue, the destruction of provincial theatre, and the Americanization of English culture.[38]

Nostalgia for the statuesque nudity of times past: the Seldoms, a once popular music-hall act who 'managed to combine a great deal of nudity with considerably more art than the nudes of today achieve'.

The Footlights Flickered forms an interesting contrast to J. C. Trewin's *The Gay Twenties* which covers the same period. To Trewin (1958) it was a time of chaotic energy – 'a decade ever ready to look at the new thing, to open astonished and delighted eyes at any fresh idea'.[39] To Macqueen-Pope (1959) people of the 'twenties 'stood on the slopes of a slippery world, a world of brittle ice, from which the old safeguards of solidity, national feeling, home life and domestic discipline had largely gone.' [40]

In his writings Macqueen-Pope, a latter-day Canute, sought to hold back the inexorable tide of modernity as demonstrated by the encroachment of mass entertainment. But it is his preoccupation with the enduring as distinct from the ephemeral which most characterizes his writings on the theatre. This applies equally to theatre buildings, public spaces, and cultural values. Hence his selection of the Haymarket, the St. James's, and Drury Lane, his descriptions of the Strand, Piccadilly, and Leicester Square. Such descriptions however brought him face to face

with the transitory and with change. For him the modern London was not 'a maelstrom of perpetual disintegration and renewal'.[41] The milk bars, cinemas, and jukeboxes of the 'forties and 'fifties represented the invasion of barbarism, an invasion which had started with the First World War, and now continued with the Americanization of English (not British) culture.

Thus it was the Edwardian era that he encased in a cocoon, to be preserved from such onslaughts – an ideal against which all further developments could be measured, a prelapsarian Golden Age. Macqueen-Pope needed to recall this age to preserve it from extinction, and perhaps to preserve himself. Vivian Ellis, who composed music for such hits as *Mr. Cinders*, described Macqueen-Pope in 1953:

Somewhere in a series of offices, in the upper circles of darkened theatres or high above the roar of the London traffic, Macqueen-Pope has always sat, rather like an extinct bird in its lofty eyrie. There he broods, surrounded with bound volumes of old plays and prints, typing, smoking, and saying how tired he is of it all, but never too tired to share a laugh, a sorrow. . . . [42]

The Age of Machinery

In *Carriages at Eleven* Macqueen-Pope was able to marginalize all manifestations of progress as quaint and insignificant ('What will they be up to next?').[43] In his later books his perspective shifted to those elements of destructiveness, which he identified specifically with the Age of Machinery. When the first bomb was dropped on English soil in December 1914, it destroyed the English cocoon of insularity. The triumph of the internal combustion engine also signalled an irrevocable change in the rhythm of life.

The leisurely pace which seemed to characterize the Edwardian era had been eroded in the theatre as well. Just as the stately pageant of Gaiety Girls had been supplanted by the more energetic eroticism of the chorus in *The Belle of New York*, so the musicals and musical comedies based on chiffon, jewellery, and waltz-time succumbed to the onslaught of revue from 1907, and to those changes in rhythm identified with modernism, such as the syncopation of 'Alexander's Ragtime Band' (1911), *Hullo Ragtime* (1912), and *Hullo Tango* (1913). By the late 'forties Macqueen-Pope's comment that *Oklahoma* had hit London 'like a cyclone'[44] was not so much a euphemistic welcome as a response to yet another over-paced onslaught from across the Atlantic.

Little awareness of any of the changes which occurred in the 'twenties stirred Macqueen-Pope's cocooned vision of the period. The most noticeable absence, however, is any awareness of the role of cinema. The first commercial exploitation of film in the West End took place in 1896, that *annus mirabilis* of popular modernity, at the Empire and, in the same year, at the Alhambra. Macqueen-Pope would have identified these as mere quaint manifestations of the search for novelty, like the aeroplane or the combustion engine. (He was later to describe how 'cinema audiences come out silently, almost furtively, as if they had been participating in secret and unholy rites, instead of enjoying themselves'.)[45]

In his last book on London theatre, *The Footlights Flickered*, Macqueen-Pope devoted a chapter to what he called '1928 – And the Great Challenge.' He was referring specifically to 27 September, when critics went to the Piccadilly Theatre for a press showing of a film, and heard Al Jolson say on screen, 'Wait a minute, wait a minute – you ain't heard nothing yet.' The veteran journalist Hannen Swaffer declared to Macqueen-Pope 'The theatre is dead . . . I have just seen it die' – and Swaffer, as Macqueen-Pope noted, immediately became a film critic as well.[46]

It was a moment of crisis: the Age of Machinery had forever changed the nature of entertainment. Moreover, the 'twenties were for Macqueen-Pope an age of disenchantment generally. The strikes and hunger marches, culminating in the General Strike of 1926, saw him acting as a Special Constable armed with a baton to fend off the striking barbarians.

The Historiographical Problem

Macqueen-Pope's books often open and close with prologues and epilogues of protest, in which post-war England is vilified for its loss of empire, its welfare state, its nationalization of industries, its lack of clear-cut social and gender divisions, the disappearance of formal dress codes, the appalling manners and appearance of the youth of the day, the Americanization of popular culture, and the harmful impact of television and film. Only in the calm and allegedly unchanging world of the commercial theatre did Macqueen-Pope find the solace he craved. And only in the period between 1900 and 1914 did he find the world of shirtfronts and sables for which he pined.

Narratives of an idealized theatrical past are the means by which his longings and his desires for a personal utopia are satisfied. But, as Susan Stewart comments, 'By the narrative process of nostalgic reconstruction the present is denied, and the past takes on an authenticity of being, an authenticity which, ironically, it can achieve only through narrative'.[47] Indeed, she goes on to suggest that nostalgia, 'like any form of narrative, is always ideological: the past it seeks has never existed except as narrative, and hence, always absent, that past continually threatens to reproduce itself as a felt lack'.[48]

This is the nub of the historiographical problem that Macqueen-Pope poses for us today. But it is also the lesson that he teaches us. For surely we must consider rather than dismiss the significance of memory and nostalgia, even in the work of such 'wistful remembrancers' as Macqueen-Pope, in any investigation of a theatrical past that must always be a melting-pot of 'imperfect recognitions' and unattainable desires.

Notes and References

1. W. Macqueen-Pope, *Shirtfronts and Sable: a Story of the Theatre when Money could be Spent* (London: Robert Hale, 1953), p. 305.

2. W. Macqueen-Pope, *Ghosts and Greasepaint: a Story of the Days that Were* (London: Robert Hale, 1951), p. 19.

3. W. Macqueen-Pope, *Twenty Shillings in the Pound* (London: Hutchinson, 1948), p. 6.

4. *Theatres of Memory: Past and Present in Contemporary Culture* (London; New York: Verso, 1994), p. x.

5. Ibid., p. 15.

6. *Hazlitt's Literary Remains*, I, p. cxx, quoted in William Archer and Robert Lowe, ed., *Hazlitt on Theatre* (New York: Hill and Wang, 1957), p. xxvii.

7. Revised edition (London: MacGibbon and Kee, 1968), p. 9–11.

8. *On Longing: Narratives of the Miniature, the Gigantic, the Souvenir, the Collection* (Durham; London: Duke University Press, 1993), p. ix.

9. *Yearning for Yesterday: a Sociology of Nostalgia* (New York: Free Press, Macmillan, 1979), p. 49.

10. *Ghosts and Greasepaint*, p. 13.

11. Ibid.

12. Ibid., p. 15.

13. *Half a Century of Entertainment* (London: Dennis Yates, n.d.), unpaginated.

14. *Carriages at Eleven: the Story of the Edwardian Theatre* (London: Hutchinson, 1947), p. 7–8.

15. Ibid., p. 8.

16. *Haymarket: Theatre of Perfection* (London: W. H. Allen, 1948), p. 46.

17. *The Anti-Aesthetic: Essays on Postmodern Culture* (Port Townsend, Washington: Bay Press, 1983), p. xiv.

18. Anne C. Colley, *Nostalgia and Recollection in Victorian Culture* (Basingstoke: Macmillan, 1998), p. 3–4.

19. Ibid., p. 4–5.

20. A. E. Wilson, *Edwardian Theatre* (London: Arthur Barker, 1951).

21. J. C. Trewin, *Edwardian Theatre* (Oxford: Basil Blackwell, 1976), p. 28.

22. Allardyce Nicoll, *English Drama 1900–1930: the Beginnings of the Modern Period* (Cambridge: Cambridge University Press, 1973). Nicoll acknowledges *Carriages at Eleven* (p. 18) and discussions of actor-managers (p. 20), refers briefly to *Gaiety, Theatre of Enchantment*

(London: W. H. Allen, 1949) and to *Nights of Gladness* (London: Hutchinson, 1956, p. 153–4), and mentions a short essay on Daly's (p. 159).

23. See Michael R. Booth and Joel H. Kaplan, ed., *The Edwardian Theatre: Essays on Performance and the Stage* (Cambridge: Cambridge University Press, 1996). In *The Revels History of Drama in English, VII: 1880 to the Present Day* (London: Methuen, 1978), p. 17, Hugh Hunt suggests, in contrast to Macqueen-Pope, that during the Edwardian era 'the country's economy was rooted in sand. Its leisurely pursuits were little more than an escape from unpleasant realities. Its social progress was achieved at the expense of uncertainty and a sense of impermanence.' A particularly challenging approach is offered by Peter Bailey, 'Theatres of Entertainment: Spaces of Modernity', *Nineteenth Century Theatre*, XXVI, No. 1 (Summer 1998), p. 5–24, who considers the notion of 'modernity' in the relationship of popular entertainment at the turn of the century to social and economic change. He evolves a concept of popular modernism, and suggests that this was the means, through popular entertainments such as the music hall and musical comedy, by which popular audiences explored anxieties around change and new developments. While Bailey believes we should remain alert to the 'countervailing and modifying power of inertia, continuity, and resistance', he also implies that there was a substantial audience for 'the stage forms of popular modernism, whose entertainments could be read as texts for living in a volatile urban world'. This call for a more complex cultural reading of popular theatregoing in the period is important, especially as historical surveys of popular entertainment in these years often represent it as stable, secure, unaffected by change and an oasis from the incursions of new technologies (which of course it wasn't).

24. *Shirtfronts and Sables*, p. 302.

25. *The Melodies Linger On: the Story of Music Hall* (London: W. H. Allen, 1950), p. 9.

26. *Shirtfronts and Sables*, p. 302.

27. *Nights of Gladness*, p. 240.

28. Ibid., p. 23.

29. *The Melodies Linger On*, p. 30.

30. *The Footlights Flickered* (London: Herbert Jenkins, 1959), p. 14.

31. *The Melodies Linger On*, p. 5.

32. *Shirtfronts and Sables*, p. 11–12.

33. Ibid., p. 300.

34. Ibid., p. 301.

35. Ibid.

36. *Ghosts and Greasepaint*, p. 322–3.

37. *Shirtfronts and Sables*, p. 306.

38. Op. cit., passim.

39. J. C. Trewin, *The Gay Twenties: a Decade of the Theatre* (London: MacDonald, 1958), p. 9.

40. *The Footlights Flickered*, p. 17.

41. Marshall Berman, *All That is Solid Melts into Air: the Experience of Modernity* (London: Verso, 1983), quoted in P. Bailey, 'Theatre of Entertainment', p. 6.

42. Vivian Ellis, 'I'm on a See-Saw', quoted by Alan Dent, 'Walter Macqueen-Pope', *Dictionary of National Biography 1951–60* (Oxford: Oxford University Press, 1971).

43. *Carriages at Eleven*, p. 7.

44. *Ghosts and Greasepaint*, p. 197.

45. Ibid., p. 321.

46. *The Footlights Flickered*, p. 198.

47. *On Longing*, p. 23.

48. Ibid.

Helen Freshwater

Suppressed Desire: Inscriptions of Lesbianism in the British Theatre of the 1930s

In this response to John F. Deeney's article, 'Censoring the Uncensored: the Case of *Children in Uniform*', which appeared in NTQ 63 (August 2000), Helen Freshwater enters the growing debate over our reclamation of historical depictions of homosexuality. She questions Deeney's contention that our contemporary critical prejudices obscure the circulation of dramatic images of lesbianism during the 1930s, proposing that the Lord Chamberlain's difficulties in identifying lesbianism demonstrate the impossibility of dispensing with the theoretical structure that informs our understanding of this identity. Her archival research also reveals that there were in fact many efforts to put the lesbian on the stage during this period, but that these were effectively suppressed by the Lord Chamberlain, who refused to contemplate the performative enactment of lesbianism, no matter how indistinct or conventionalized in form. Her article addresses the challenges faced when addressing these dramatic inscriptions of lesbian desire, which are often homophobic, prurient, and unquestioning in their affirmation of the heterosexual norm. Helen Freshwater has recently completed her PhD on performance and censorship in twentieth-century Britain at the University of Edinburgh, and now lectures in drama and performance at the University of Nottingham. Her 'The Ethics of Indeterminacy: Theatre de Complicite's *Mnemonic*' appeared in NTQ67. She is also a contributor to the *Edinburgh Review* and to the anthology *Crossing Boundaries* (Sheffield Academic Press, 2001).

JOHN F. DEENEY'S article 'Censoring the Uncensored' provides a useful corrective to the orthodox line which proclaims that 'the beginning of lesbian theatre was in 1975'. Furthermore, his investigation into the successful production of Christa Winsloe's play, *Children in Uniform*, effectively illustrates the distortions created by reading theatrical history from a critical perspective coloured by contemporary preoccupations. However, John Deeney concludes that 'the existence of Winsloe's *Children in Uniform* does not necessarily suggest that there are numerous other dramas from the period in question discoursing lesbian passion'. Further research into the archival remnants of this period reveals that these lost and buried dramatic images do exist, but also highlights the difficulty of discarding our critical conditioning following their excavation.[1]

There can be no doubt that the history of the lesbian has been characterized by silencing, denial, invisibility, and erasure; and that this makes researching the dramatization of lesbianism a particularly laborious task. Deeney's reclamation of *Children in Uniform* begins the work of unearthing a submerged mountain of material. While *Children in Uniform* has never been a canonical text, it was published, produced successfully, and garnered substantial media coverage. But accessing material that did not enjoy similar attention or success naturally proves more problematic. It seems that many plays that reflect lesbian subjectivity or experience have been effectively excised from history – subjected to the 'censoring impulse' Maggie B. Gale foregrounds in her introduction to *West End Women: Women and the London Stage, 1918–1962*.[2]

Jill Davis assesses the difficulties created by this critical repression in her introduction to the first published anthology of British lesbian plays, observing: 'When plays are not published they disappear from history and little is left to a future generation of theatre historians and practitioners.' And she concludes:

In editing this volume I would like very much to have included a play by, about, for lesbian women written before 1945. I haven't found one. I am not surprised, since theatre is the most public of all art forms and I doubt that such a play would have received a licence for performance. Having failed to receive a performance its chances of an after-life, through publication, are small.[3]

This article will show that, during the early 'thirties, there were many attempts to place lesbianism on the stage. However, as I will illustrate, any search for a play 'by, about, [and] for lesbian women' rests upon several flawed hypotheses.

The Death of the Playwright

Davis's criteria for inclusion display all the signs of critical blindness that Deeney is so keen to remedy. Her agenda demonstrates the essential incompatibility between projects that seek to reanimate positive role-models from a lost lesbian past and those that are merely interested in uncovering the dramatic discourse surrounding lesbianism. None the less, it is important to recognize that *any* revisionist criticism that aims to reclaim women writers and their work as lesbian is fraught with complexities and contradic-tions. These difficulties are not exclusive to critics who openly equate the personal and the political, or literature and liberation. Problems arise the moment one attempts a definition of a 'lesbian text'. Can it only qualify as a 'lesbian text' if it has a lesbian author? Does a lesbian play require a lesbian playwright? Or indeed lesbian characters?

Reina Lewis addresses this issue in her essay 'The Death of the Author and the Resur-rection of the Dyke', in which she expresses her consternation at the critical tendency to 'reread texts exclusively in the light of their authors' (newly discovered) homosexuality'.[4] She claims that this type of research often creates narrow readings which focus exclus-ively on the textual inscription of lesbian identity:

An osmosis is set up in which writers known/ suspected to be lesbian are found to have in-cluded lesbian scenes or characters in their work

(the interpretation of which can now be validated on the grounds of the author's own sexual orien-tation); in return, incidents which are interpreted (or clearly marked) as lesbian are seen to throw a new light on authors previously regarded as heterosexual.[5]

Recent criticism such as Richard Dyer's re-reading of Winsloe's work and Lynda Hart's analysis of Lillian Hellman's *The Children's Hour* acknowledges the limitations of this approach, but fail to move beyond it.[6] Hart laments the fact that *The Children's Hour*, the most canonical of all lesbian plays, is so deeply homophobic. Nevertheless, she states that it 'must be considered in its historical moment', and concedes that we must avoid imposing our own expectations upon a text written in 1934. However, she then follows up with a contradictory proviso:

I want to point out that Hellman chose to show the play's events from the perspective of the homophobic community. A lesbian writer might have found subversive ways to affirm the relation-ship, whereas Hellman simply kills Martha off.[7]

Hart's efforts to promote these two incom-patible opinions indicate the impossibility of her position, and the ultimate pointlessness of all attempts to dust off unrecognized les-bian authors as part of a project of political affirmation.

There are indications that some critics are moving away from preoccupation with the lived experience of the writer. Reina Lewis suggests that we cease searching for undiscov-ered lesbian writers and heroines in literary history, and accept that this history has a con-tradictory and often uncomfortable nature. She proposes that we focus our interpreta-tions on 'the texts themselves, including those that are unsympathetic or written by men, as a transcript of society's attitudes to lesbians and women'.[8]

Alan Sinfield echoes Lewis's call in *Out on Stage*. He recommends that we stop wasting valuable time and energy on speculation about the sexuality of the playwright, and spend it on analyzing performance, repre-sentation, and imagery instead. He comes to the same conclusion as Lewis:

There is no correlation between the (reported) sexuality of the writer, director, or performer and the way he or she represents homosexuality. On the one hand, lesbians and gay men have produced hostile representations, because that was how they saw themselves, or that was the best they could manage in those conditions, or they needed to work. . . . Queer history is not just that which we have made for ourselves and it is not composed only of positive images. We might chart the situation on two axes: in/visibility and un/friendliness. Very often, representations scoring high on visibility would score low on friendliness; in fact, until recently there was a direct correlation: the more hostile a representation, the easier for it to claim visibility.[9]

It appears that the real problem for lesbian criticism lies in the resistance of dramatic representations, such as *The Children's Hour*, to efforts to recuperate them as part of a project of celebration or belated recognition. As we shall see, dramatic images of lesbian desire created during the first half of the twentieth century are often homophobic, prurient, and deeply conventional in their reinstatement of the heterosexual norm.

Invisibility and Emergence

Any attempt to resurrect the work of forgotten lesbian playwrights from the first half of the century is in danger of missing one of the most important points about the history of homosexuality: the fact that this concept was only just emerging during the early twentieth century. Famously, the House of Lords voted to reject a bill designed to criminalize lesbianism in 1921. Lord Desart, the Director of Public Prosecutions, voiced his opposition to the Bill on the grounds that: 'You are going to tell the whole world that there is such an offence, to bring it to the notice of women who have never heard of it, never thought of it, never dreamt of it. I think that is a very great mischief.'

The Lord Chancellor was of the same opinion, declaring: 'I would be bold enough to say that of every thousand women, taken as a whole, 999 have never heard a whisper of these practices.'[10] The very discussion of lesbianism, even for an act of public prohibition, was considered more dangerous than

the benefits of control and containment through legislation. The public appears to have been largely unaware of female homosexuality before this period, or at least had never heard it named. The opinion of the theatre critic, St John Irvine, illustrates this perception of public naivety. Writing in 1933, he hypothesized: 'I doubt if there was one person in a thousand who, before 1914, knew the meaning of the world Lesbian.'[11]

This climate of ignorance helps to explain the confusion of the Lord Chamberlain's readers when confronted with *Children in Uniform*. As Deeney notes, the censorship's Advisory Board were unsure if *Children in Uniform* actually represented lesbianism at all. However, the Lord Chamberlain's decision to err on the side of leniency was uncharacteristic. Between 1930 and 1935, his office banned five plays outright for representations of lesbianism which were, for the most part, both highly conventional and extremely oblique.[12]

The Lord Chamberlain's treatment of *Love of Women*, written by Aimée and Philip Stuart in 1934, is representative. His decision to ban the play came as a surprise to the couple, who had previously enjoyed a string of West End hits, including *Her Shop* (1929), *Nine Till Six* (1930), and *Sixteen* (1934).[13] Aimée Stuart wrote to the Lord Chamberlain in protest, asking him to give the matter his personal consideration:

This is a very serious matter for us. We earn our living by our work and can't afford to waste it. . . . Ours is a delicate play – entirely on the side of conventional morality – about two women, who, because of the shortage of suitable men, live for work, for ideas, for friendship![14]

The play's focus upon these two young women, Vere and Brigit, illustrates one of the main problems the censorship faced: a script's ambiguity. The reader who produced the initial report on the play pronounced: 'Unfortunately the whole play is dubious, to say the least, and one of the most difficult to report on I have ever had.'

This difficulty is reflected in the many contradictory statements occurring throughout his report. First he declaims, 'homosexuality between two women is much of the theme', only to add the proviso: 'It does not exist but it is talked about.' He then contradicts himself completely: 'Lesbianism is never mentioned. . . . The girl['s] advance is Lesbian, but that could easily be cut out.' He brushes past these glaring inconsistencies (lesbianism is 'never mentioned', but 'it is talked about'; 'it does not exist', but the girl's 'advance is Lesbian') to draw the conclusion that the Lord Chamberlain should not licence the play due to its 'atmosphere'.[15]

The play then went to the Advisory Board, where questions about its performance were raised. The script was one thing, and the potential for the play to build on 'atmosphere' or inference in performance quite another. Lord David Cecil reported back:

This play is a borderline case: but on the whole I think it should not be licensed. It is true . . . that homosexuality is not ostensibly a motive of the action. But it hovers in the background of much of the dialogue, and would be more obtrusive in actual performance than in reading.[16]

Here the readers and advisors ignored questions of authorial intent to concentrate on a much more important issue: the audience's reception of the work. Anxiety over the communicative potential of connotative content, or the realization that the audience might well interpret the work in an entirely different manner to the censor, disturbed the Lord Chamberlain's staff. Having contemplated the subjectivity of every such reception, the disquieting instability of performance added to the censorship's worries.

Decoding and Definition

Confusion over *Love of Women* was such that a further report from reader Henry Game raised the question of the censorship's policy on the depiction of homosexuality. The staff of the censorship office hardly ever mentioned 'policy'. It was generally accepted that things were to proceed in an *ad hoc* fashion, and each play was to be read 'on its merits'. However, Game insisted:

The problem really boils down to one of policy. If any mention of perversion on the stage is taboo,

then this play cannot be allowed. If on the other hand perversion can be mentioned, then this play where it exists merely as a rumour can be judged on its general intention, which is wholly moral, and could pass.

Game finally concluded that any discussion of such 'perversion' should be kept off the stage, no matter what the authors' intention:

To sum up: the play is a harmless and even moral play, but it does introduce perversion as a factor in the plot and this gives an advertisement, in the emotional atmosphere of the Theatre, to a fact of life which it would seem undesirable should be discussed in public. My opinion . . . is that the taboo should be maintained.[17]

Part of the confusion may have been caused by the Stuarts' anticipation of the censor's unsympathetic reaction to any mention of lesbianism. When the play was given a short private production in June 1935 the suspicion that the authors had employed a degree of self-censorship was articulated by W. A. Darlington, who reviewed the play for *The Daily Telegraph*:

There is interesting stuff here; but to be developed properly the whole case would have to be discussed in such detail as the Censor would surely never allow. Hampered by this official shadow, the authors skirt uneasily but inoffensively round their subject.[18]

By the time the play toured to New York at the end of 1937, the overall judgement of the American reviewers was that *Love of Women* had been so much watered down as to have become unintelligible. *Variety* reported that the play 'flies over, under, and around the Lesbian theme, but never alights directly on it'.[19] The reviewer for the *Sun* noted: 'It is always possible, incidentally, that someone has been doing house cleaning on the play, and left behind the confusion and muddle characteristic of house cleaning.'[20] Another critic, Richard Watts, Jr., damned the play as 'a hollow and aimless work that has been so carefully cleansed of its dangerous sex matters that it has lost whatever dramatic point it may once have possessed'.[21]

These reviewer's comments have some validity. *Love of Women* reveals lesbianism one minute, only to obscure it the next. It goes to considerable trouble to justify the women's unconventional domestic arrangements, as the characters explain at length that their commitment to each other is about work and companionship, not sex. The play labours the point that male shortcomings rather than any 'abnormality' on the women's part have brought about this situation.

It seems that this defence is necessitated by a radical shift in the perception of intimate female friendships. In *Surpassing the Love of Men*, Lillian Faderman contends that love between women was presented in positive terms in the cultural sphere until the 1920s. She indicates that the freshly-labelled 'New Woman' was often depicted as turning to romantic friendship as the alternative to heterosexual coupling, but that initially no shame or reticence attached to these relationships.

The Stereotype of the Spinster

The contemporary response to Vere and Brigit would undoubtedly have been conditioned by earlier dramatic enactments of the New Woman. Viv Gardner traces the proliferation of this image of nascent feminism in *The New Woman and her Sisters*, a collection dedicated to the analysis of this theatrical figure. Gardner remarks that this character's literary debut in 1894 was greeted with some hostility.[22] The New Woman's espousal of progressive notions, adoption of emancipated habits, and severe dress-sense undoubtedly presented a radical subversion of normative femininity.

Gardner concludes that her commitment to education and financial independence was interpreted both as a rejection of a reproductive role and a challenge to masculinity; and consequently the New Woman became an object of satire, vilification, and ridicule in the mainstream drama of the 1890s. However, none of the contributors to this volume detect any association of the New Woman with lesbianism in these early attacks. The definition had no social significance in the 1890s: the emergent discourse of sexology had begun to identify and label the female 'invert', but the general public had yet to do so.

In her essay, 'The New Woman and the New Life', Jill Davis acknowledges this disjunction, noting that at the time, 'the social persona of the lesbian had not yet issued from the discourse of sexology into cultural reality and could not therefore be "represented".'[23] This disequilibrium could not last for long. Faderman notes that images from the 1920s left the Victorian model of female asexuality behind. What would have been dismissed as an innocent friendship in the 1890s is recognized and labelled as lesbianism. This categorization was clearly negative. The lesbian was figured as a neurotic abnormality or a peculiar outcast.

Davis notes that female autonomy gradually came to be equated with the figures of the 'frustrated' spinster, the 'selfish' barren wife, and the 'predatory' lesbian in popular culture, while Faderman suggests that this social opprobrium was the result of increasing anxiety over women's developing social and economic independence. She states:

Romantic friendships, which might have been viewed as harmless to the heterosexual status quo, thus became increasingly threatening since many women no longer had to marry for the sake of economic and social survival alone. Romantic friendships could potentially take the place of marriage on a scale much larger than what had before been possible.[24]

Faderman and Davis's work is supported by other critics who highlight the replacement of Victorian sexual mores with a resexualization of women. As George Chauncey, Jnr., observes, this served to fuel condemnation of the celibate or disinterested woman, and effectively tied women to 'heterosexual institutions such as marriage'.[25]

The presence of this ideology in *Love of Women* has been emphasized by Maggie B. Gale, who proposes that the play reflects the longevity of pre-First World War attitudes towards spinsters. She comments that many social theorists and sexologists during the inter-war period continued to promulgate the notion that if 'a woman was intentionally single and desired economic and personal independence . . . there was indeed something "wrong" with her, that in fact she wasn't a "natural" woman'.[26] This is the very belief that disturbs Vere and Brigit's blissful, pre-lapsarian arrangement. Their autonomous existence is curtailed by society's refusal to accept the two women's definition and explanation of the relationship. What has changed between the 1890s and the 1930s are the terms of the disapprobation they face.

The shifting pressures surrounding the categorization of female same-sex relationships demonstrate the complexity of any definition of lesbianism, historical or otherwise. The Lord Chamberlain and his readers may well have had trouble identifying the lesbian in this play, but the question of definition is no less problematic today. Our interpretation of the nature of the relationship at the centre of *Love of Women* is still conditioned by contemporary definitions of lesbianism, and the very circumstances of reception which so concerned the censor.

For example, the critical emphasis of women's studies in the 'seventies would thus have encouraged the reading of Vere and Brigit's relationship as 'woman-identification'. Adrienne Rich's influential essay, 'Compulsory Heterosexuality and Lesbian Existence', advocated a broader definition of lesbianism, and a revalorization of female friendship and comradeship, introducing the idea of the 'lesbian continuum'. Vere and Brigit's intimate companionship certainly registers on this continuum, as reference to Rich's definition reveals:

I mean the term *lesbian continuum* to include a range – through each woman's life and throughout history – of woman-identified experience, not simply the fact that a woman has had or consciously desired genital sexual experience with another woman. If we expand it to embrace many more forms of primary intensity between and among women, including the sharing of a rich inner life, the bonding against male tyranny, the giving and receiving of practical and political support . . . we begin to grasp breadths of female history and psychology which have lain out of reach as a consequence of limited, mostly clinical, definitions of *lesbianism*.[27]

Rich's redefinition was not greeted with universal enthusiasm. Some lesbian critics were unhappy with a definition of lesbianism that attempted to elide or obscure the importance of physical expression and sexual practice. Eve Kosofsky Sedgwick explores this idea in *The Epistemology of the Closet*. She maintains that for many pro-sex feminists, an approach such as this seemed 'to expose a devastating continuity between a certain, heretofore privileged feminist understanding of a resistant female identity, on the one hand, and on the other the most repressive nineteenth-century bourgeois constructions of a sphere of pure femininity'.[28]

What this debate reveals is the importance of acknowledging our unavoidable cultural conditioning. Vere and Brigit could have been interpreted as New Women at the turn of the century, radical lesbian separatists during the 'seventies, or as sexually repressed and self-deluding today. No critic can hope simply to dispense with the theoretical structure that informs our understanding of the word 'lesbian'. The label does not indicate a fixed term, but a definition being pulled to and fro in a conflicted space of opposing and contradictory forces.

Lesbian Panic, Conventional Climaxes

Dealing with these contingencies, as well as with ambiguity and obscurity, is an inevitable part of any historical assessment of the dramatization of lesbian desire. During the twentieth century, gay and lesbian identities were initially informed by representations that were furtive, ambiguous, and largely hostile. We may not be able to retrieve positive depictions of lesbianism from the pre-1945 period, but there is no shortage of disturbing imagery available for analysis and interpretation – or of unhappy endings.

Love of Women thus draws to a predictably miserable close. Brigit leaves to marry a dashing young doctor, and the curtain falls on Vere, distraught and alone. Both *Children in Uniform* and *The Children's Hour* conclude with suicide, as did another play censored by the Lord Chamberlain in 1934. This piece, *Lady of the Sky*, written by Gilbert Wakefield, finishes with the spectacular demise of the eponymous heroine, who ends her independent existence by wilfully crashing her plane.

Playwright Nina Rapi stresses that these melancholy endings are a common theme in the representation of lesbianism, since the lesbian is invariably assigned the role of the tragic heroine who succumbs to madness or commits suicide. Rapi divides plays between works written *by* lesbians for a lesbian audience, and plays written *about* lesbians by heterosexuals for a general audience. She proposes that, in the latter,

the lesbian is inevitably presented as desiring but not desired. Being viewed from the outside, she is perceived and represented as 'imitation of men, psychological regression, a seduction of other women, a blasphemy or a perversion, a 'sexual preference', a fascistic hard-line feminist, a pity.[29]

However, Rapi's distinction between plays written *for* lesbians and plays written *about* them is based on a spurious connection between author, text, and audience. The multiple contingencies of production and reception mean that any attempt to base a critical judgement upon the sexual orientation of the author, or indeed, the audience, is a pointless exercise.

The obscurity of much of the censored material buried in the Lord Chamberlain's Plays and Correspondence Archive further undermines the grounds for such an inquiry, as the use of authorial pseudonyms confounds judgement based on the playwrights' sexuality or, indeed, their gender. Without the trail of biographical information left by famous or celebrated authors, the name on the script can tell us very little about the source of the material.[30] Moreover, Rapi's categorization cannot account for those plays which were denied performance. Here, the connection between a work and its contemporary audience is permanently broken.

None the less, Rapi's identification of the consistently negative portrayal of lesbianism on the stage seems accurate enough, and other critics confirm this overwhelmingly negative representation. Patricia Smith's identification of what she terms 'lesbian panic' certainly appears to apply to these plays:

Typically, a female character, fearing discovery of her covert or unarticulated lesbian desires – whether by the object of her desires, by other characters, or even by herself . . . lashes out directly or indirectly at another woman, resulting in emotional or physical harm to herself or others. This destructive reaction may be as sensational as suicide or homicide, or as subtle and vague as a generalized neurasthenic malaise. In any instance, the character is led by her sense of panic to commit irrational or illogical acts that inevitably work to the disadvantage or harm of herself and others.[31]

Sadly, there was clearly little alternative for a lesbian character caught within the restrictions of theatrical realism in the early 1930s.

However, Deeney's article is representative of a gradual critical move towards the rehabilitation of such realist strategies.[32] He suggests that the miserable conclusions of plays such as *Children in Uniform* may be recuperable, proposing that this play 'succeeded in creating a lesbian space within the heterosexual paradigm of realism'. He places his faith in the process of performance, and speculates that the play's enactment may have enabled a partial reinscription of a position of traditional subordination.[33]

However, it is difficult to reproduce such positive thinking when faced with the successful suppression through censorship of other plays during the 1930s. As audiences never had the chance to witness them, no one was given the opportunity to question their conventional conclusions. Of course, the censor's decision to ban plays with commonplace climaxes – such as *The Children's Hour*, *Love of Women*, and *Lady of the Sky* – might be taken as a sign of their latent potential for subtle subversion. However, reference to the Correspondence files reveals that the censorship was often convinced of their conservatism, and chose to ban them regardless.

For example, the Lord Chamberlain was clearly in agreement with Hart's verdict on the homophobia of *The Children's Hour*. We might expect his perception of its conformity to recommend the play to him, but this was not the case. The Lord Chamberlain's Office was prepared to acknowledge Hellman's conventional stance, but this made no difference to their final judgement. A letter from the office to Hellman's producer, Hugh 'Binkie' Beaumont, reads:

There are, of course, degrees of the presentation of unnatural vice, and in this play *Children's Hour*, it could not be more delicately handled, as indeed one would expect from a playwright of Miss Hellman's eminence and reputation. The play does not centre round this attitude, which is anyhow shown as deplorable, nor indeed do the principals practice this vice – the reverse – but it is introduced into the play and therefore the Lord Chamberlain cannot give the play a licence.[34]

It is important to remember that this diplomatic missive was carefully written for public consumption. However, even in private the Lord Chamberlain was prepared to acknowledge the difference between a play's content and its tone. Passing judgement on *Lady of the Sky*, he had ruled:

The play may not be technically either indecent or demoralizing, still . . . no matter what attempts are made to conceal it, this play's motif deals with one aspect of homosexuality, albeit the manner of presenting the theme is not offensive or blatant. Still, the germ is there and either in its female or male form I have no intention of seeing it fostered on the British stage if I can prevent it.[35]

Thus, the slightest inference of lesbianism was sufficient to justify suppression in the early 1930s. Having acknowledged the existence of lesbianism, the Lord Chamberlain would not contemplate any performance of lesbian desire on the public stage, no matter how indistinct or conventional its presentation.

Uncensoring the Censored

Both Sinfield's book and Deeney's article provide refreshing challenges to the idea that homosexuality was either unspeakable or invisible on the stage during the early twentieth century. However, Deeney's reiteration of Sinfield's assessment of the role of the censorship is more problematic. Sinfield observes: 'By controlling irregular sexuality the Chamberlain did not eliminate it; on the contrary, he implied that it was always about to irrupt into visibility. He was helping to make theatre a place where sexuality lurked in forbidden forms.'[36] This may be true of the staging of male homosexuality, but such a reading is in danger of negating the very real impact of the censorship on the dramatic representation of lesbianism. Any discussion of British theatre is incomplete without an examination of the elements that were denied performance. Whilst censorship imposed on theatre history by a contemporary critical agenda is clearly undesirable, we might also wish to consider the value of reconsidering plays which were effectively silenced before they reached the stage: 'uncensoring the censored', perhaps.

Notes and References

1. John F. Deeney, 'Censoring the Uncensored: the Case of *Children in Uniform*', *New Theatre Quarterly*, No. 63 (2000), p. 219–26 (p. 225).
2. See Maggie B. Gale, *West End Women: Women and the London Stage, 1918–1962* (London; New York: Routledge, 1996), p. 2.
3. Jill Davis, ed., *Lesbian Plays* (London: Methuen, 1987), p. 9.
4. Reina Lewis, 'The Death of the Author and the Resurrection of the Dyke', in Sally Munt, ed., *New Lesbian Criticism: Literary and Cultural Readings* (New York; London: Harvester Wheatsheaf, 1992), p. 17.
5. Ibid., p. 23. Focus on a playwright's sexual identity as a key to interpretation ignores the fact that a production of a play is a communal effort, and that an entire team of producer, director, designer, and performers also contribute to theatre's execution. What is more, an author-led interpretation is often only possible when dealing with canonical material. The lives of Hellman and Winsloe have attracted biographical attention and coverage, which encourages investigations into the relationship between their lives and their work. This impulse is confounded when dealing with obscure works written by unknown authors.
6. Richard Dyer, *Now You See It: Studies in Lesbian and Gay Film* (London: Routledge, 1990).
7. Lynda Hart, 'Canonizing Lesbians?' in June Schlueter, ed., *Modern American Drama: the Female Canon* (London; Toronto: Associated University Presses, 1990), p. 275–92 (p. 290, n).
8. Lewis, 'The Death of the Author', p. 26.
9. Alan Sinfield, *Out on Stage* (London; New York: Routledge, 1999), p. 3.
10. Cited by Jeffrey Weeks, in *Sex, Politics, and Society: the Regulation of Sexuality since 1800* (London: Longman, 1981), p. 105.
11. St John Irvine, cited by Richard Findlater, *Banned* (London: MacGibbon and Kee, 1967), p. 141.
12. Restrictions of space curtail discussion of the other two, namely *Alone*, by Marion Norris, banned in 1930, and *Riviera*, by Henry Broadwater, banned in 1935.
13. See Maggie B. Gale, *West End Women*, Appendix, p. 198–237.
14. Aimée Stuart, letter, Lord Chamberlain's Correspondence file, British Library Manuscripts (LC Corr.), 4 June 1935.
15. George Street, report, LC Corr., 27 October 1934.
16. Lord David Cecil, letter, LC Corr., n.d.
17. Henry Game, report, LC Corr., 4 June 1938.

18. W. A. Darlington, 'Marriage or a Career: Old Conflict in a New Play', *The Daily Telegraph*, 2 June 1935. The play ran for three performances from 2 June 1935 at the Phoenix Theatre, London, where Margaret Webster directed the Repertory Players.

19. 'Love of Women', *Variety*, 15 December 1937. See Kaier Curtin, *We Can Always Call Them Bulgarians: the Emergence of Lesbians and Gay Men on the American Stage* (Boston; London: Alyson, 1987), p. 221–2.

20. Richard Lockridge, 'The New Play', *New York Sun*, 14 December 1937.

21. Richard Watts, Jr., 'The Theaters', *New York Herald Tribune*, 14 December 1937.

22. Gardner states: 'The New Woman was first named, it is claimed, by the radical novelist, Sarah Grand, in the *North American Review* in May 1894.' See Viv Gardner, in *The New Woman and her Sisters: Feminism and Theatre 1850–1914*, ed. Viv Gardner and Susan Rutherford (London; New York: Harvester Wheatsheaf, 1992), p. 3–4.

23. Jill Davis, 'The New Woman and the New Life', in *The New Woman and her Sisters*, p. 25.

24. Lillian Faderman, 'Love Between Women in 1928: Why Progressivism Is Not Always Progress', in Monika Kehoe, ed., *Historical, Literary, and Erotic Aspects of Lesbianism* (New York; London: Harrington Park Press, 1986), p. 23–42 (p. 28).

25. George Chauncey, Jr., 'From Sexual Inversion to Homosexuality: Medicine and the Changing Conceptualization of Female Deviance', *Salmagundi*, No. 58–9 (1982–83), p. 114–46, (p. 144).

26. Maggie B. Gale, *West End Women*, p. 186.

27. Adrienne Rich, *Blood, Bread, and Poetry: Selected Prose 1979–1985* (London: Virago, 1986), p. 51.

28. Eve Kosofsky Sedgwick, *The Epistemology of the Closet* (New York; London: Harvester Wheatsheaf, 1991), p. 37.

29. Nina Rapi, 'Hide and Seek: the Search for a Lesbian Theatre Aesthetic', *New Theatre Quarterly*, No. 34 (1993), p. 147–58, (p. 155), including quote from Harriet Ellenberger, 'The Dream is the Bridge: in Search of Lesbian Theatre', *Trivia*, No. 5 (Fall 1984), p. 53.

30. Marie Stopes's use of several pseudonyms (including George Dalton and Clifford Cooper) illustrates this problem. See LC Corr. files for *Married Love*, 1923, and *Cleansing Circles*, 1926.

31. Patricia Juliana Smith, in *Lesbian Panic: Homoeroticism in Modern British Women's Fiction*, ed. Lillian Faderman and Larry Gross (New York: Columbia University Press, 1997), p. 2.

32. For example, Gale refers us to Sheila Stowell, who suggests that the traditional perception of realism as a hegemonic form needs challenging: 'This position raises a number of problems, beginning with its assumption of a simple and direct relationship between reproduction and reinforcement. While genres or styles . . . may not be politically neutral, they are surely capable of presenting a range of ideological positions. . . . Dramatic forms are not in themselves narrowly partisan. They may be inhabited from within a variety of ideologies.' See *A Stage of Their Own: Female Playwrights of the Suffrage Era* (Manchester: Manchester University Press, 1992), p. 100–1. See also Maggie B. Gale, 'Women Playwrights of the 1920s and 1930s', in *The Cambridge Companion to Modern British Women Playwrights*, ed. Elaine Aston and Janelle Reinelt (Cambridge: Cambridge University Press, 2000), p. 23–37, and 'Errant Nymphs: Women and the Inter-War Theatre', in *British Theatre Between the Wars 1918–1939*, ed. Clive Barker and Maggie B. Gale (Cambridge: Cambridge University Press, 2000), p. 113–33.

33. Deeney, 'Censoring the Uncensored', p. 224.

34. Norman Gwatkin, letter, LC Corr., 27 March 1946.

35. Earl of Cromer, comment on report, LC Corr., 23 February 1935.

36. Alan Sinfield, 'Private Lives/Public Theatre: Noël Coward and the Politics of Homosexual Representation', *Representations*, No. 36 (1991), p. 43–63.

Ewa Obrębowska-Piasecka and Juliusz Tyszka

Meetings by the Lake: on the Tenth Anniversary of the Malta Festival

The Malta of this feature is not an island surrounded by sea but a lake surrounded by land – the artificial lake created near the Polish city of Poznań for the World Kayak Championships of 1990. However, since that event, and the momentous political changes with which it coincided, the lake has become the annual focus for a quite different event: a festival of theatre that has earned a reputation for both hosting and initiating important experimental work which is none the less rooted in the need to maintain close contact with its ever larger and more enthusiastic audiences. A range of illustrations of some of the oustanding productions accompanies retrospects by two regular members of those audiences – Juliusz Tyszka, who outlines the origins and development of MALTA, and Ewa Obrębowska-Piasecka, who offers a personal response to the achievements of the festival and to the philosophy of theatre underlying them.

Juliusz Tyszka

A Few Grandiose Observations

TWELVE YEARS AGO, in the spring of 1989, the word 'Malta' was associated in Poznań not so much with the beautiful island in the Mediterranean as with a huge, cheerless grey excavation that became the artificial lake of that name (water having been released into it a few years earlier), lying about two kilometres as the crow flies from the centre of the town.

The excavation and its surroundings had been one of the many deserted, neglected, always litter-strewn, seemingly unproductive areas around Poznań. Then suddenly, in the space of a few months, water appeared once again in the lake, above it sprang the buildings and infrastructure of a recreation and sports centre – earth-shattering changes in the cause of the World Kayak Championships which the town and sports authorities had fought some years before to hold in Poznań in 1990.

Despite huge obstacles (the biggest of course being lack of funds), and thanks to the superhuman efforts of the organizers, along with assistance from the administration, the investment was completed in time. The championships were held, medals were awarded, and the canoeists left, destined for professional assignments elsewhere in the world. Above the Malta lake remained the buildings and the accompanying trappings of tourism and recreation, erected under the momentum of the preceding events. There also remained the question of what was to be done with them.

It was then that the city administration considered turning the Malta area into a recreation centre for the inhabitants of Poznań. One of the means of enlivening the Malta environment and bringing it closer to the Poznań public was to be a modest festival of open-air theatre, like the couple of dozen such events regularly taking place in Europe – one of the first on the Continent, the International Festival of Street Theatre in Jelenia Góra, in South-Western Poland, having been initiated by Alina Obidniak in 1983. MALTA was to take place in June every year, during the International Trade Fair in Poznań, thereby substantially enhancing the city's artistic attraction for trade fair guests.

And so, between 11 and 16 June 1991, seven theatre groups from Poland, Italy, and

Spain presented eight performances – three in theatre spaces, five in the meadows by the Malta lake and in the old town square. The festival turned out to be a success, with the number of spectators for performances near Malta outnumbering the fans at the first league football matches during the time of Olimpia Poznań. Most important of all, the older residents of the city welcomed with great curiosity and the younger with unconcealed enthusiasm the new forms of contact with theatre – outside conventional theatre buildings (encountered fairly rarely), free, and with crowds who were friendly towards the performers, in expectation of good fun and perhaps a significant artistic experience.

There were many organizers of the first Malta Festival who helped to animate it by their goodwill and energy, chief among these the administrative director of the festival, Michał Merczyński (a manager, then not quite thirty, working at the Teatr Polski), and its artistic director, Grzegorz Mrówczynęski. A vital role in this and the following MALTA was also played by the legendary group, Teatr Ósmego Dnia (Theatre of the Eighth Day), which had just returned to the country after several years of exile enforced by the communist regime. Ósmego Dnia performed their open-air show *Mięso* (*Meat*) in 1991 and put the festival organizers in touch with their foreign contacts, thanks to which three groups came to Poznań – Teatro Nucleo and Teatro Tascabile from Italy, and La Burbuja Teatro from Spain.

The same programme formula and scale of festival was preserved during the following year. It is important, however, to note that the second festival took place in the middle of July, thus severing the relationship with the Poznań Trade Fair. MALTA was already standing on independent ground.

The creators of the festival quickly began to reap rewards from their initiative: the success of the first MALTA encouraged, for example, a young student group in Poznań, the Teatr Biuro Podróży (Travel Agency Theatre), to prepare for the next festival the premiere of an open-air performance – the unforgettable *Giordano*, with Andrzej Rzepecki, who is unfortunately no longer with us

today, in the title role. The triumph of *Giordano* during the second MALTA opened the doors of the theatre world to this group.

In 1993, with the third MALTA, a fundamental change took place, when Lech Raczak – following his departure from the Teatr Ósmego Dnia, which he co-founded in 1964, and led from 1968 to 1993 – was appointed artistic director of the event. The producer of MALTA '93 was, for the first time, a private artistic agency – TAFF ART, founded in 1992 by Michał Merczyński and Włodzimierz Mielcarek. From this moment to the present day MALTA has become – thanks primarily to these three people, and later also to Renata Borowska – a model of modern cultural management on a truly national scale. It is here that unconventional developments in the field are tried out, later to be taken up by institutes of culture throughout the country. MALTA follows in the path of its joint creator and director, for the institutions where Michał Merczyński works are its producers.

To the expanded mainstream programme of MALTA '93 was added a fringe festival, with Włodzimierz Mielcarek as director of 'MALTA Off', and the event was moved to late June through early July (as it turned out for good). Among the MALTA premieres of that time were the *Carmen Funebre* of Teatr Biuro Podróży, *Merlin* by the Towarzystwo Wierszalin (Wierszalin Society), *Uczty duchowe* (*Spiritual Feasts*) by Akademia Ruchu (the Academy of Movement), and *Sabat* (*Sabbath*) from Teatr Ósmego Dnia.

Concentrated encounters with the theatre – most of them of an alternative, experimental kind, in unconventionally arranged interiors of theatre halls – were accompanied by mass fun and games, or else by silence amidst the unvoiced admiration of the several thousand spectators gathered in the open air.

In turn, MALTA '94 initiated a formula that has proved its value over seven years and which the festival maintains today – one that has led to exceptional success on the European scale for the Poznań event. In the space of five days it offered to the public 18 performances and live actions from 15 groups in the main programme and some 30

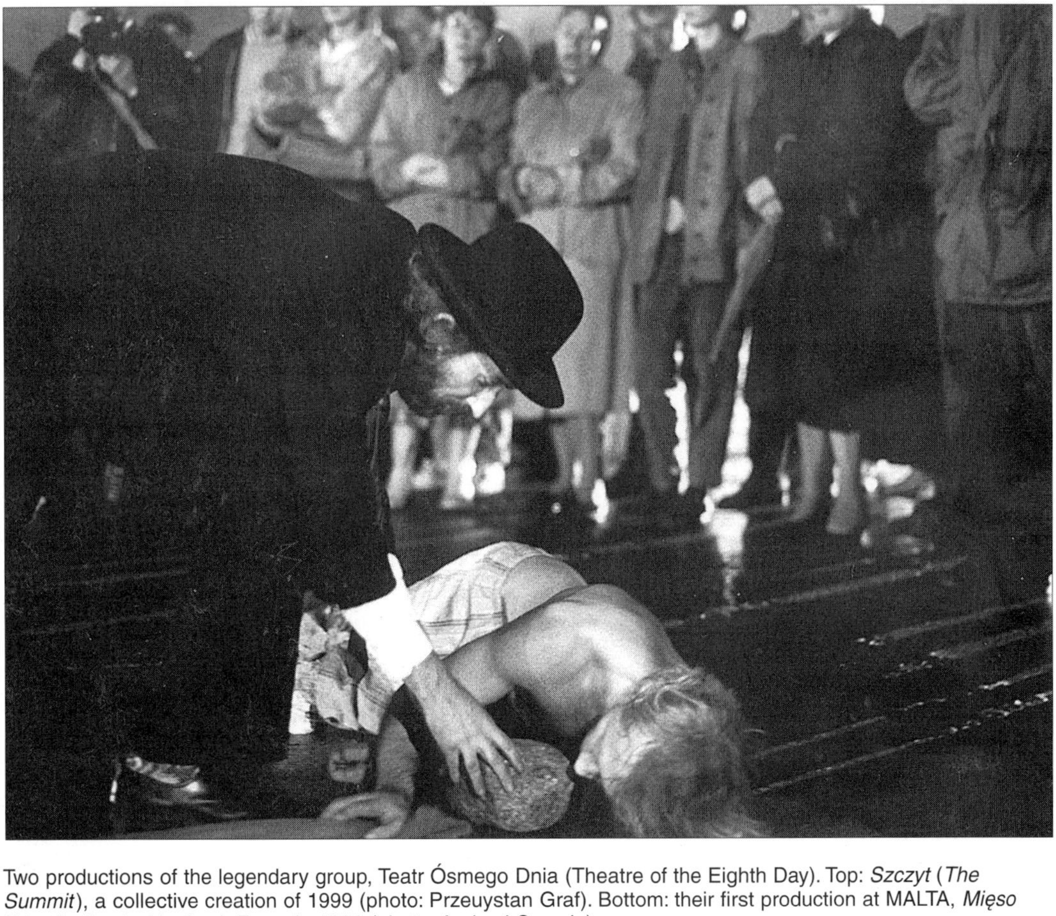

Two productions of the legendary group, Teatr Ósmego Dnia (Theatre of the Eighth Day). Top: *Szczyt* (*The Summit*), a collective creation of 1999 (photo: Przeuystan Graf). Bottom: their first production at MALTA, *Mięso* (*Meat*), directed by Lech Raczak, 1991 (photo: Andrzej Szozda).

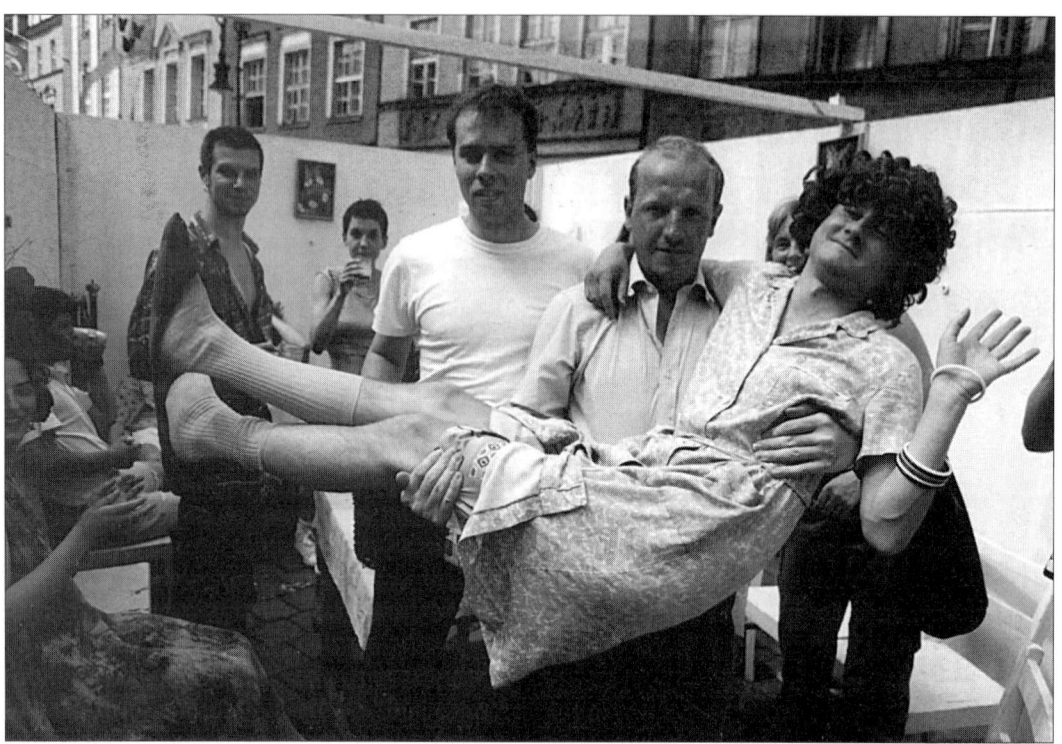

performances by 28 groups in the 'Off' pro-gramme – plus 8 performances from 6 groups in a newly created part of the festival entitled 'Poznań at MALTA' – 97 shows altogether. MALTA '94 was thus a disappointment only to theatre-lovers who wanted to see every item on its varied programme, and who instead had to practise the difficult art of choosing.

In summing up the first five festivals, Michał Merczyński, who had been from its very inception the moving spirit of the event, noted some of the basic ideas and assumptions underlying the MALTA project in the *Kronika Miasta Poznania* (*Chronicle of the City of Poznań*). These included:

1. The rehabilitation of city spaces degraded in their cultural functions after forty years of subservience to institutional culture.

2. The creation of a desire amongst the public for more open forms of participation in culture, in keeping with the inspiriting slogan 'Open Air Art = Democratic Art'.

3. The making from the festival of a 'theatre sacrament', in which the prime movers were not only the performing artists but rather (and perhaps even primarily) the thousands of spectators as co-creators.

4. The creation of a contemporary form of democratic *polis*, with the festival a contributing to the broadening of the social functioning of Poznań.

Among the ways in which these aims were to be achieved were:

1. The choice of performances on the grounds of their unconventional use of scenic space, whether indoors or in the open air.

2 Support and inspiration for unconventional artistic projects and their creators.

3. The co-production of premieres by selected Polish and European companies whose artistic profiles were in accord with the principles of the festival

4. Inspiration and support for the artistic initiative of young groups from Poznań. The most significant example in this respect has been the success of Teatr Strefa Ciszy (Zone of Silence Theatre) and its presence at MALTA every year from 1994 to 2000.

Two companies from Poznań. Opposite page: Teatr Strefa Ciszy's production of *Judasze* (*Judases*) at the 1995 festival (photo: Andrej Andrejczsk). This page: Teatr Biuro Podrózy, in (top) *Giordano*, 1994, and (bottom) *Selenauci* (*Moonwalkers*), 1999 (photos: M. Kowalczyk, Bogusław Biegowski).

The combination of these efforts is to be found in the harmonic connection, both in the programme and in organizational activities, between the many functions of MALTA in terms of art, cultural creation, tourism, and economics. To the means of realizing the objectives formulated by Merczyński were added, in succeeding years, that of engaging the media (especially television) in the work of the festival and in creating from MALTA programmes for the media on a national scale.

In this manner the revolutionary changes then taking place in Poland found their expression in the creation of MALTA which, in the space of ten years, achieved enormous significance, real and symbolic, in all aspects of its work. Its size and the scale of its role in cultural creation is demonstrated today not only in numbers (100–130,000 spectators during every year of the festival since 1994), but in the impatient anticipation of theatre-lovers (especially the young) for the next MALTA; in dozens of original artistic initiatives; in radical and influential theatrical and organizational innovations; and last but not least in the generation of a feeling of togetherness in a joyous crowd, freed from aggression, and geared towards the shared experience of something vital.

This is precisely the role of MALTA in the creation of culture and of value. Although it tries not to allow itself to be entrapped by neat sociological and anthropological formulations, this is what is most often emphasized in reviews of the Poznań happenings. And it was during the 1990s at this very festival that a clear form was given to the longing of Poles for a 'live' meeting of substance with other people which would simultaneously be an occasion for the renewal of universal values. MALTA also became an important occasion for several thousand spectator-citizens of a country that was finally free, enabling them to meet together in mutuality and to attempt better to define their present identity. All this was thanks to the art of theatre, in its more unconventional, experimental forms.

In every epoch, but especially in times of tumultuous social change and fundamental historical shifts, the need for large gatherings of people manifests itself in many places and contexts. The fullest and clearest manifestations of this occur amongst crowds participating in spectacular events. Theatre is the most interesting of spectacles since it offers the fullest and most accessible possibilities of uncovering the truth of our emotions and the direction of our thoughts, of guiding the development of our values. We recognize these things intuitively – during the joyful remembrance of play, in the gasps of breath when moved which we share with the spectators we discover around us, and most of all with the people on stage who have thus provoked our feelings.

During the past century huge numbers of spectators abandoned the theatre in favour first of the cinema and then of the television screen. Theatre was thought by many critics and theorists to be a disappearing art, no longer needed by people. However, in contrast with the cinema and television, the theatre holds its trump card, as an unmediated face-to-face meeting between actors and spectators, giving those spectators influence over the course of the event. The emotionally charged understanding between actors and spectators is what allows theatrical performances to take flight, and gives birth to vital happenings even when the artistic level may not be of the highest.

Such vital encounters between actors and audiences become legendary and find their place in history. Sometimes they may occur only once in a lifetime, and during MALTA many people have lived through something of this nature. Theatre will last as long as people want to meet with each other in order to seek out the truth about themselves and the world through unmediated contact.

A great deal depends, however, on conditions – on the kind of circumstances that theatrical institutions create for the encounter between actors and spectators. For more or less four decades we have observed in world theatre a searching for new forms of such contact, in order to free both actors and spectators from the burdensome and oppressive mediation of institutions and institutional spaces (most of all, theatre buildings with proscenium stages), and thereby abandoning conventions of acting as well as of audience

Theatre in a steelworks. One of the unconventional venues used during the Malta festival. Above. the Centrum Sztuki Teatr Dramatyczny from Legnica are seen in their 1997 production of *Zły* (*Bad*). Photo: Maciej Rusinek.

Above: Teatr Strefa Ciszy's open-air production of *Wodewil Miejski* (*City Vaudeville*), 1996 (photo: Marianna Michałowska). Opposite page: Goran Bregović and musician from *Wedding and Funeral Band*, 1997.

behaviour. With ever-increasing enthusiasm and boldness, actors are preferring to meet their spectators in the open air – in fields, on the streets – or in circus tents, factories, warehouses, or even odder places where, in the opinion of the animateurs, there is an opportunity for a vital, authentic meeting with an audience.

There is a re-animation of the traditions of popular theatre, the theatre of fairs, the kind of 'illegitimate' theatre that was previously relegated to the margins of official life – equally opposed by the secular and spiritual authorities. Contemporary creators of drama and theatre such as the 1997 Nobel laureate Dario Fo, uncovered for a twentieth-century public the forgotten traditions of commedia dell'arte, of medieval tumblers, or tellers of magical tales. And the public 'buys' this, filling thousands of meadows, squares, streets, gigantic halls, and stadiums. The laboratory stream of theatre develops simultaneously,

following the example of great twentieth-century experimenters such as Constantin Stanislavski and Jerzy Grotowski, trying to develop new means of contact with their spectators.

MALTA has drawn together all the tendencies in this laboratory stream of theatre, knitting together in Poznań, in the Poland of the 1990s, a shredded social fabric. May it continue to be a great laboratory of the culturally creative function of theatre in a drastically changing society. May it continue to bestow the benefits it has given to all of us – whether theatre-lovers, casual passers-by, critics, managers, artists, tramps, children of the Old Town, or crowds of walking spectators at Malta – who impatiently await the next theatrical feast at the high point of summer.

Translated by Jolanta Cynkutis
and Khalid Tyabji

Ewa Obrębowska-Piasecka

I, You, He, We, They: Some Nostalgic Reflections on MALTA

THE MALTA FESTIVAL was born at a very specific moment of transition in Poland and for Poles. At the beginning of the 1990s we were still hungrily swallowing our newly acquired freedom. We were impassioned by the television coverage of parliament (where members expressed exactly what they thought in grammatically correct Polish), we read papers from front to back (a world, formerly known to us only through autopsy, but now related without resort to the official mumbo-jumbo of our former epoch). We strongly believed that life could be beautiful, truly ours.

I write 'we' because this was truly a phenomenon of common experience. I write 'we' because then it was truly unnecessary to have special meetings in special circles to experience a sense of togetherness. The tram, the pavement, the university, the place of work, were sufficient. Truly self-governing structures were born – new and independent media, ways of business quite unknown until then. However critically one may look at those years today, there appears – as with almost every former time – a note of nostalgia, linked with the prams on which street-hawkers arranged 'soaps and jams', the first pubs, and the fact that it was finally possible without any great problems to travel to the West.

The feeling of being together, however, lasted only a short while. The consequences of change also occasioned losses, the disintegration of institutions and structures, as the shared system of values and beliefs stemming from a common source, which had led people to the barricades against the old regime, were polarized before our very eyes. 'This is the Right, this the Left, this is Black, this Red.' And the 'we' not coming into play at all. Battles began over power, money,

influence, careers. Masks fell, faces were revealed. They were not always beautiful. Ordinary citizens interested themselves more and more with their personal privacy – not with great social affairs or revolutionary ideas, only with peace of mind.

In this duality – of joyful exultation on the one hand and the beginnings of disillusionment with the new reality on the other – MALTA made its appearance. It has remained until today the untarnished child of its times. It has matured as reality itself has changed, while simultaneously revealing the transformations – sometimes through metaphorical means, by way of its choice of performances, at other times in a straightforward manner – giving rise to lively and contrasting reactions amongst journalists, politicians, and spectators alike.

The early 1990s were also an important time for the theatre – most of all, a difficult time. The realities of the market determined that there was not sufficient money to go round. The all-pervading 'freedom' reduced Melpomene to the level of one amongst the many arts. One must remember here that in the reality of communist times the relation between the stage and the audience was of a very specific character in Poland: the theatre was its bastion of independence, the place for the exchange of clandestine (*read:* forbidden) ideas. Now this was no longer expected from it by anyone: it was possible to express freely, anywhere, whatever one thought. Financial difficulties combined with the reduced prestige of a theatre whose actors and directors were no longer the high priests of society resulted in enormous frustration. As usually happens in such situations, some fell into torpor whilst others set out in search of new directions, developments, and inspirations.

It is not surprising that MALTA sought out artists pursuing the second option. It rapidly became evident that the festival not only blazed its own trail but signalled the direction if not for the entirety then for several of the streams of contemporary theatre in Poland. What is important is that this was not only an artistic but an organizational and economic direction besides.

In repertory theatres, artists complained when there were empty seats. In order to fill them they buttressed themselves through performances of school texts and low-level comedies. State subsidies vanished from sight, so salaries shrank, scenography was minimal, and of music specially composed for a production there was no mention at all. The then Ministry of Art and Culture – steered *nota bene* by a theatre director of long standing – decided that it would not continue to support all the existing institutions, and there lurked the menace of liquidation or the danger of the unknown passage to a position of self-governance. Terror was in the air – coupled with the reflection that the theatre's plight was nothing when compared with the threat to medical services, education, the very budget itself. In such a context the artistic condition of theatres did not encourage any struggle over the issue of their continuance.

The situation amongst the independent theatres was no happier, as they also experienced the talons of the market. Those that depended on official institutions (most often of higher education) were no longer able to count on funding. And those that were self-supporting found themselves surrounded by competition. The feeling in general circulation was that this was the twilight of the 'off' stream of theatre – one that had been identified primarily with social and political engagement. What, asked the sceptics, was the use of a militant theatre if there was no one to fight against? More radical voices were heard which questioned the use of any kind of theatre in a world changed by television, video, and the internet.

In this rather dismal context the success of MALTA appeared to be an authentic miracle. Please try to imagine a huge, empty, area on the outskirts of a large city. There is nothing there – no shops, no cafés, not even benches or garbage bins. Darkness, eyes straining to see as soon as dusk falls. Singly at first, seemingly unsure, residents of the city are making their way from the centre of town in the direction of regatta finishing-posts. Those who have already arrived sit in the few dozen chairs laid out for them. They wait, as yet not knowing for what. Their number grows steadily while all along the shores of the lake can be seen yet more streams of pilgrims in their path who, reaching the escarpment, take their places behind the backs of those already seated.

Then, in absolute darkness, the voice of Lech Raczak – narrator of the performance, *Quixoté* by the Italian Teatro Nucleo – rings out. I shall not forget this moment till my dying day – my memory layered with the uncommonly poetic, intelligent, and joyful nature of this performance. And as for the crowd, it would be improper so to designate the people who – without tickets, plush

Another scene from Teatr Strefa Ciszy's open-air production of *Wodewil Miejski* (*City Vaudeville*), 1996.
Photo: Marianna Michałowska.

seating, or evening dress, but with reverent attention – participated in this artistic event. However many times MALTA may be relegated to the fairground stream of theatre, this memory will reawaken in me. This was not the ludic entertainment of a herd, rather the truest form of theatrical magic.

I unfailingly return to this initiation with enormous sentiment and nostalgia. In the pioneering days of MALTA, in the most simple way in the world, I fell in love with the festival. I must, however, hasten to add that this was not at all an easy love.

MALTA was a phenomenon which fascinated ordinary spectators as well as sophisticated theatregoers, though over time the former fitted themselves into it more readily than the latter. Michał Merczyński, director of MALTA, often said that this was a democratic festival. Since such catch-words are easily lapped up by newspapers, I instantly sold it. It was the same with the information that MALTA attracted more spectators than premiere league football matches. The difficulties became apparent only when I began

personally to experience democracy amidst the growing crowds.

I remember the transition during which MALTA grew to monstrous proportions as a most painful experience. 'A hundred performances in the space of a few days? But no one can possibly see them all!' I cried. I was furious also when, for the umpteenth time, I was unable to see anything other than the backs of those who had reached a production ahead of me. There were two options open to me: to be offended by MALTA and return, for instance, to the 'normal' theatre – or to learn to live with it, and learn to function within it.

It is clear that I chose the second option. I was no longer bent on seeing everything: firstly, I chose performances according to personal criteria; secondly, I left if I found that the space for spectators was arranged in such a manner that I could not see anything. I took the risk that I may miss something of importance, but such a risk was not mine alone. I learnt about a new context of theatre, and artists learnt about it too. It was fascin-

Teatr Ósmego Dnia's production of *Sabat* (*Sabbath*), 1993. Photo: Maciej Rusinek.

ating to observe how, from year to year, young groups got increasingly better in their mastery of the space and of the crowds: how, without abandoning any important aspect of their performances, they extended the boundaries of theatre.

It paid off to wait for consecutive performances by the Biuro Podróży, Strefa Ciszy, Komuna Otwock, and the legendary *Okna* (*Windows*) of the Teatr Prób (Theatre of Trials – but in Polish also Theatre of Rehearsals) from Wągrowiec, in order to see how reper-

tory theatres operate at MALTA – not merely transplanting 'root and branch' productions that had been created for conventional stages, but 'going the whole hog' (Węgierko Theatre from Białystok) or else into factory hangars (Modjeska Theatre from Legnica).

Democracy expressed itself not only in statistics but also in scale – and in the variety of artistic and conceptual propositions. To get such propositions accepted was not easy. First to question them were the politicians. A group of rightist councillors protested against

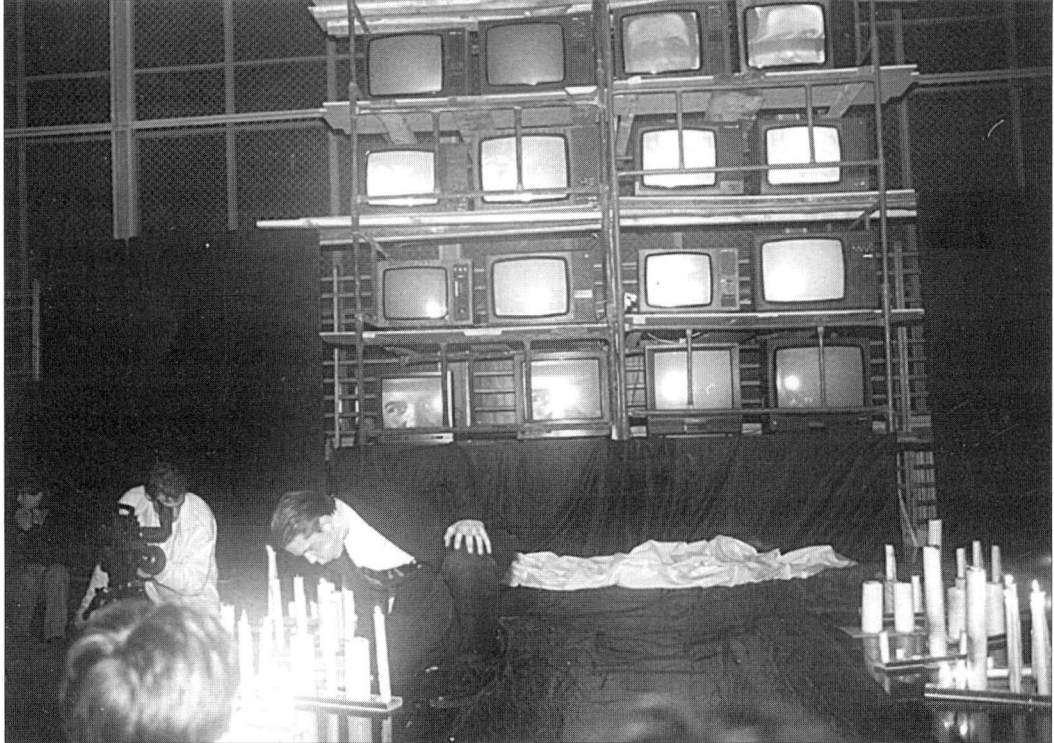

Two scenes from the production of *Okna* (*Windows*) by Teatr Prób (Theatre of Trials – in Polish also meaning Theatre of Rehearsals), 1994. Photos: Marek Siłacz.

what was (in their opinion) seditious in a performance by the group Turbo Cacahuete. The French made their way through the town with a coffin, looking in at a hospital and a butcher's shop in the course of their meanderings. They entertained the spectators by trying to express, in this manner, their opinion about funeral ceremonies. The councillors denounced them as sacrilegious and insulting. A debate was set in motion in the media – about art, and about life.

Journalists were also divided. I remember an unholy row when, in the columns of a single paper, there appeared two reviews devoted to a performance by the Spanish group, La Fura Dels Baus. The reviewer of the national edition wrote of 'Total Theatre' whilst his colleague of the local supplement saw 'Totally Nothing'. And so began a time of discussions, controversies, polemics, ever more solidly grounded, not instigated by any higher authority but forged in the heat, straight after performances, and carried into pubs, into homes, into the editorials of newspapers, into academies, into trams. People lived theatre, and theatre pulsated in life.

To date those most difficult to convince about MALTA are the serious theatre theoreticians and historians. It is true that those among them unafraid of the difficult conditions of being a spectator in the open air penetrate into and write about the world of its performances, finding in it interesting, substantial fare for theatrical and historical inquiry. Others – and I am not accusing them all of succumbing to home comforts and comfortable thoughts – decided that at MALTA there was, very simply . . . no theatre.

And of course not every one of MALTA's presentations deserves serious attention. I am afraid, however, that theatrical purism leads to throwing the baby out with the bathwater. It is easy to cling to the carnivalesque image of MALTA. We see clowns, stilt-walkers, and fire-eaters. There are flaming towers and sinking ships. There are parades with loud music and fireworks. I understand that those most familiar with Shakespeare and Chekhov may experience a certain lack of relish. But Shakespeare and Chekhov are present at MALTA as well, in company with Artaud

and Grotowski. They have abandoned their paper decorations and have dusted off their costumes. They appear sometimes in circus tents, wandering on tightropes and waving from trapezes, and sometimes the star-filled sky may serve as their theatrical horizon. They halt sometimes in the quadrangles of the town or in the Old Square. Having been neglected by audiences, they have brought themselves to those audiences in order to debate once again with God but in their presence about human nature and the condition of the world, the direction of theatre and the misdirections of art, to enchant with beauty and appal with ugliness. In order that people may laugh and cry. In order that the world may be better and wiser.

It is surely for this that actors exist – whether they have passed through the state schools of theatre or have worked with masters of the profession outside the bounds of the academy. Those who think that there is no respect for work here are mistaken. Quite the opposite – physical and intellectual strength coalesce into one. If one despises something, one's views must be grounded in accepted standards and a well-formed conceptual scheme. It is here that blunders, lack of understanding, and discomfiture arise – all the more painful in that they are based on the instant criticisms of an audience which, when it is not enamoured, simply moves elsewhere.

Detractors claim that the MALTA public craves frivolity and that it is easy to draw by means of such bait. Nothing of the sort. In fact my own impression is that the ambitions of the repertory theatres are significantly lower than those who have taken part at MALTA. I also have other – quite pleasant – feelings that ribald humour and spectacular theatrical effects are not accorded top value here. On the contrary: the MALTA public, having already witnessed great combustions and great subversions, simply revolts when someone tries to serve them up yet again.

My intention is not to convince anyone that the contemporary life of the theatre is exhausting itself here at MALTA, or that this festival is of itself sufficient. Far from it: I think, rather, that this is a very vital beginning. The MALTA crucible gives birth to new theatre groups and new theatrical ideas. It is these – whether we like it or not – that will determine the shape of theatre in the new century.

We are already witnessing the influence of the festival on the development of our national theatre scene. New festivals of a similar nature were created in the wake of its example. Though not on such a scale, nor with such an impetus towards realization, they none the less provide excellent contexts (not to say market opportunities) for the advancement of street theatre, open-air theatre, and other forms of exploratory theatre. And groups created here go on to travel with their performances into the world. I believe that they have much to offer. If we are delighted by the successes in Paris of performances by Krystian Lupa created in the Stary Teatr, let us also be happy with the next tour of Biuro Podróży, Strefa Ciszy, and Cinéma.

Thirdly, the MALTA experience brings about a change in the expectations of spectators and enhances their theatrical appetite and critical sense in relation to traditional theatre as well. It makes familiar the new aesthetics, as avant-garde forms of expression enter into general circulation. The gulf between experimental artists and the recipients of their offerings in society does not widen. Art does not exist in a void. All this while the traditional theatre trembles in its state of ossification – the conclusion not being that we should all be going into the streets, climbing onto stilts, and learning to juggle with knives, but simply that we should think afresh about theatrical space, about actors' training, about repertoire.

It is of some significance that the ideas of theatrical reform going back at least a hundred years have been more eagerly adopted by independent theatres than by respectable institutions. The state of the latter reminds one too often of the nineteenth-century star system. This is especially sad at a time when the surrounding reality achieves unprecedented acceleration, demanding ever new languages and means of description. This is not about the multiplication of forms, but about creative inspiration, and even more about creative debate. The emphasis on the word 'creative' demands freedom from hurt pride, and no little lack of humility. Participation in MALTA, just reading and writing about it, has been for me an altogether important experience – valuable and inspiring not only in a professional sense, but also as a private human being. In this wonderfully chaotic melting-pot – glimmering, ever-changing, and noisy – I have tried to find myself: my system of values, my expectations with regard to people and the world, my emotional and intellectual needs.

I have also – not without pain – had to open myself to others. This has not always been welcome or acceptable. However, in the circumstance of general respect for the rules of theatrical meeting, in situations governed by certain conventions, this came about much more readily than in the actuality of real life. Theatre, unchangingly, is a guarantee of the maintenance of social ties, which – at a time when contact between people has been reduced to a minimum – emerges as its greatest value.

Each time I am afraid that in this crowd I shall not find myself again. And each time I experience a pleasurable surprise, because it happens that opposite me stands a person. He looks different from me, thinks differently from me, believes in something else, but has come to talk. I don't have to agree with him, but neither do I have to contend with him. It is sufficient that we listen to each other.

I think, perhaps naively, that it is this meeting that is important for other MALTA spectators as well. Even if I am mistaken, it is something I would like to hold on to as long as possible. I would like to submit myself to this magic when, in the middle of the night, several thousand people look with concentration at one place. From this place radiate beams of thought which one may be entertained or be moved by – emotions that one will not forget till the end of one's life because of having experienced them in unison. This is 'only' theatre. But oh, what theatre.

Translated by Jolanta Cynkutis
and Khalid Tyabji

Susan Carlson

Portable Politics: Creating New Space for Suffrage-ing Women

A few of the plays written in support of the movement for women's suffrage in Britain before the First World War have recently been recovered and published, but most of these were intended for some kind of professional or at least conventional production. Susan Carlson is here concerned to look also at some of the pieces which saw print only in the ephemeral suffrage press, and production (if at all) only as part of meetings or demonstrations. Breaking down traditional distinctions between social, political, and theatrical spaces, she argues that all were part both of the dramatization of the struggle, and also of a broader reclamation of public spaces for women, whether of a public venue such as the Albert Hall, outdoor spaces such as Hyde Park and Trafalgar Square – or the humbler and lonelier space of the street corners on which women sold the suffrage newspapers that contained the plays – some of them about women on street corners selling suffrage newspapers. . . . Susan Carlson is Professor of English and Associate Provost at Iowa State University. Her books include *Women and Comedy* (University of Michigan Press), and she has recently published essays on Aphra Behn, Timberlake Wertenbaker, Shakespeare, and nineteenth- and early twentieth-century women playwrights. This essay is part of a longer study of British suffrage theatre and its connections to Edwardian productions of Shakespeare's works.

LISTEN TO the gusto with which women made their claim to social, political, and theatrical space during the most heated years of the British suffrage campaign. A suffrage journalist, writing of Ellen Terry's feminist reformulations of Shakespeare's heroines, proclaims:

> Experience teaches us that there are no bounds to the predatory instincts of the revolutionary women of to-day! They would appropriate all territories; they would plant their banner upon every high vantage ground of thought and action which history and literature bid us reverence; they would discover in all great impulses that have ever moved their sex something with which their own revolutionary spirit can claim kinship and from which it can draw perpetual inspiration.[1]

As this century opened, women in the London theatre wanted new territory, knowing full well that an expansion of space – social, political, as well as theatrical – had to accompany their reformulation of the ideological landscape. In the specific realm of suffrage theatre, women refashioned two kinds of space. First there was the monu-mental space of the city itself, London, the world's first industrial city. Women understood that in this city they were disadvantaged; as Elizabeth Wilson theorizes, women's presence in cities had always 'been questioned, and the controlling and surveillance aspects of city life have always been directed particularly at women'.[2] Nevertheless, women campaigning for the vote made the city a prime performance space and created an urban, city-inspired, mass theatre for women – an amazing, unprecedented accomplishment.

In the process of claiming such a public space, the women also reshaped a second space – the specific locations for theatrical performance. With their guerilla theatre, they found stage space in West End restaurants and on Hyde Park scaffolds, they performed politics at garden parties and in labour halls, they commandeered lavish West End theatres as well as city streets. To paraphrase Virginia Woolf, on or about 1910, theatre space changed in London, as the women who had created the British suffrage theatre proved that theatre performance was a powerful tool in the cause of political change.[3]

I would like to pause over two studies of women and stage space which provide a cautionary starting point. Hanna Scolnicov promises big results with the title of her book, *Woman's Theatrical Space*. But while her insights on Greek and Roman theatre are particularly keen, her argument is skewed by her neglect of women playwrights. She tells us that 'questions of the theatrical space thus become the question of woman',[4] but her millennia-long sweep of western theatre leads her to conclude that we have progressed past the special link between women and space (p. 154).

As I will detail later, for early twentieth-century British women playwrights, as well as for most playwrights of this century, such a dissociation is untenable. We very much need to continue our work to understand women's connection to performance space. While Una Chaudhuri's *Staging Place: the Geography of Modern Drama* is not specifically focused on gender issues, she offers a more useful theorizing of twentieth-century stage space with a focus on 'the problem of place'[5] and the ways in which 'home' and 'otherness' define twentieth-century theatre spaces.

Theorizing Women's Theatre Space

Most important for me is both authors' decision to ground their study of twentieth-century theatre in analysis of Ibsen and to note that the space of the home is central in early twentieth-century theatre; their agreement on the pivotal place of turn-of-the-twentieth-century theatre is enhanced, however, by looking at other useful strategies for making sense of the spaces – both domestic and public – which informed the theatre of early twentieth-century London.

Not surprisingly, both Scolnicov and Chaudhuri analyze Ibsen's plays to note, first, how his drawing rooms are used to define character; and second, how that space is highly problematic for women. Chaudhuri proclaims Ibsen's home spaces to be representative of what she terms 'geopathology', and Scolnicov notes that his critique of social

structures exists in a room which is 'the gilded shell of an impossible social decorum, a pretence and an imposture that attempts to cover up the vacuity of the underlying moral justification' (p. 107).

In his study of the gendered spaces of architecture, Aaron Betsky elaborates on the ramifications of the middle-class domestic interior we in theatre studies can so easily link to Ibsen. He stresses that the nineteenth-century middle-class interior drew its significance from the confining of women to a domesticated and cultivated space cut off from the freedoms of the street. It was a space of interiority, 'a place where you turned back to yourself, rather than appear on the stage of the world'.[6] The space was, simultaneously, a fantasy, a synthetic vision of women's bifurcated social life; but importantly, the unrealistic construction (and constriction) of domestic space also promised a kind of liberation for women. As Betsky puts it,

The resulting realities created a new stage for women, a place that was potentially empowering and imprisoning, a place of their own that was tied to the networks of change, a place that was both isolated and allowed women to create a new world. (p. 142)

(His use of a theatrical metaphor is telling.) Out of the powder-keg of the drawing room, then, women did indeed cultivate the power which would lead to new social, cultural, and political freedoms. And as European women capitalized on their situational opportunities, and moved beyond the domestic cage, they undertook a struggle to define both public and private space: 'Thus the city became the embodiment of the struggle for power between men and women, played out in terms of how the city should work, appear, and grow' (p. 148).

Elizabeth Wilson reminds us that as long as women were represented by the domestic interior, the public world could be defined to exclude them. In her study of nineteenth-century London, she, like Betsky, notes the double nature of women's definition by and in the city, but she focuses on the streets, not the drawing room. She notes that women are supposedly excluded from city streets at the same time the regulations of city life develop from a fear of women on the street.

> There is fear of the city as a realm of uncontrolled and chaotic sexual licence, and the rigid control of women in cities has been felt necessary to avert this danger. Urban civilization has come, in fact, to mean an authoritarian control of the wayward spontaneity of all human desires and aspirations. Women without men in the city symbolize the menace of disorder in all spheres once rigid patriarchal control is weakened. That is why women – perhaps unexpectedly – have represented the mob, the 'alien', the revolutionary. (p. 157)

Such theorizing of women in the oppositional spaces of the domestic interior and the public street suggests that women's reshaping of space in the city would have to draw from and destroy the patriarchal divisions and definitions of space.[7]

For the women who built the suffrage theatre of early twentieth-century London, such considerations of urban space had to be factored into their political strategies. To borrow from Lorainne Code's useful terminology, women had to destroy their 'underclass epistemic status' and discover a space in which they could command 'epistemic authority'[8] as they campaigned for the vote. And according to sociologist Henri Lefebvre, the women had no choice about finding such new space: to effect revolutionary change, the suffragists had to create new space.

> A revolution that does not produce a new space has not realized its full potential; indeed it has failed in that it has not changed life itself, but has merely changed ideological superstructures, institutions or political apparatuses. A social transformation, to be truly revolutionary in character, must manifest a creative capacity in its effects on daily life, on language, and on space. (p. 54)

In the rest of this essay, I would like to show that the women who fought for and in the suffrage theatre did exactly that: produce new space. They offer a clear and exciting example of women claiming political, cultural, and epistemic authority by claiming previously unavailable space. Unapologetically, these women claim propaganda as their artistic medium and their right. The

playwright Cicely Hamilton proclaimed in 1909 that suffragists 'had started a new system of propaganda by means of plays, that was so successful that everybody was trying to steal the plays or imitate them in some way'.[9] And such propagandistic plays demanded new performance spaces.

Morphing Space

The mutability of performance space is the defining quality of suffrage theatre. This theatre cannot be attached to specific spaces or places, but exists in a guerilla-type relation to perceived places of power. As a result, suffrage playing-space challenges the comfortable boundaries of private and public as well as conventional understanding of the gendered quality of such spaces.

Most students of suffrage theatre history will be familiar with the most radical campaign tactics of the English suffragettes: their prison hunger strikes (and the retaliatory forced feedings), their breaking of windows and torching of country homes, their disruption of public events from parliamentary debate to theatre performances, their attacks on public art. These were the most sensational of the suffragists' attempts to claim public attention.

But in their theatre also the suffragists' omnipresent reclaiming of space is groundbreaking. In the pages that follow, I have grouped the women's remaking of performance space in three categories. The first two – the spaces of suffrage newspapers and the spaces of public rally – find women taking their performances to new and unprecedented locations. In the third category – actual theatre performances – I hope to show how even the conventional stage was reformulated as a performance space when suffrage politics were primary.

I Suffrage Newspapers and City Streets

In 1912, it was possible to purchase one of four hefty weekly suffrage newspapers in London: *The Common Cause* (organ of the National Union of Women's Suffrage Societies, NUWSS); *The Vote* (organ of the

Women's Freedom League, WFL); *Votes for Women* (originally the organ of the Women's Social and Political Union, WSPU, and later of the United Suffragists); and *The Suffragette* (organ of the WSPU after 1912). More important, you could buy these papers *on the street from women*. Those editing the papers, in fact, mounted massive efforts to get women on the street corner selling papers. Suffragists standing on urban street-corners in London selling feminist, political newspapers was clearly a claim to space (both public and epistemic) traditionally withheld from women.

A cursory glance at the newspapers turns up regular encouragement for women to take on this disruptive public assignment. Even in the most conservative, *The Common Cause*, a dignified and upbeat plea for help is evident: 'Excellent results are being met with by those who sell the paper outside (and where permissible inside) meetings of special interest to women. . . . To sell the paper is to propagate our Suffrage policy everywhere, and to keep the public informed of our activity.'[10]

The more aggressive politics of the WFL and the WSPU translated into a continual though still gentle hype about the need for sales. Charlotte Despard, leader of the WFL, pleads to her readers, 'our circulation must go up', and recommends that members spend their 1913 Christmas holiday in 'all parts of the country' selling copies.[11] WFL sales 'organizer' Ethel Fennings names particular street corners that have proven receptive to direct sales, and her detailed figures about circulation suggest the gritty work involved in this journalistic hawking:

Wednesday and Friday I canvassed sympathizers and others, and was successful in selling one or more copies of *The Vote* in every case, and also obtained two regular subscribers, while others promised to consider the matter. There are many other little ways of helping, and I shall be so glad to hear from any, even those who can only give the smallest amount of time. Will sympathizers in Balham please write to me soon?[12]

But *Votes for Women* mounted perhaps the most intense efforts, with regular articles on efforts to gain new subscribers and higher sales. In 1911 the paper notes 'another 141 new readers' and urges a continued recruitment effort in spite of 'the boycott with which the London press has been trying to defeat our movement'.[13] A plea in February 1913 notes record sales, the co-operation of newsagents, as well as the political necessity of 'building up a politically educated public opinion so necessary to the triumph of an idea for which a great political battle is being waged'.[14] And, later in 1913, *Votes for Women* sellers laid claim to both the street and new readers in a Christmas Poster Procession in which 'each member of the procession bore three lanterns and boards with Christmas decorations, all in our colours. . . . Papers sold well along the route.'[15] Even women on summer holiday were urged to follow the example of Miss K. S. Birnsingl, who posted *Votes for Women* posters on the landing stage of her summer Thames bungalow.[16]

The Plays in the Suffrage Press

This subtle though constant pressure was also incorporated into the propagandistic plays which appeared in the newspapers. In their journalistic staging, the plays suggest the social battering women took on the street at the same time as showing women in the process of claiming new rhetorical and public space. While these pages were a somewhat fleeting and highly disposable venue for publication, the women (and men) writing such plays had the advantage of almost instant turn-around in the publication of their work. The political goal of encouraging campaigning clearly came before dreams of literary longevity.

The most fitting example of a newspaper play which encouraged this new street-life for women is *Su' L' Pavé*, Gladys Mendl's two-column play about 'Half an Hour in the Life of a Paper-Seller'.[17] The play's heroic paper-seller, named fittingly 'Suffragette', has only the play's first and last lines. She begins by hawking papers, '*Votes for Women, Votes for Women*, one penny!' and ends by selling her last copy for gold! In between her two lines, as she sells at least twenty copies of the paper, a parade of passers-by – from children to Tory women, from Americans to Scotsmen, from dustmen to rich persons – comments on her, her politics, and the general direction of the campaign.

The seller is asked to absorb a good deal of battering, from the taunts of children to off-colour propositions to haughty disdain. But she is also treated to support – a Constable says he buys the paper, a taxi-driver calls out his support, and a retired draper notes, 'I owe everything to the ladies.' The crowd is a mixture of those clearly supporting the vote (ten persons), those clearly against (twenty-one), and those who simply want to abuse or use a woman alone on the street (seven). The result is what feels like a fairly realistic portrait of the unpredictable give-and-take of the street-life of the woman paper-seller. One 'Be-feathered lady' calls out, 'You've no right to stand out there in the wet, selling your disgusting paper' and restates the generally accepted social code: respectable women do not belong on the street and can expect social estrangement as a result.

In three other newspaper plays, the rough treatment the street paper-seller receives is replayed in broader situations in which suffragettes are doing public campaigning on the streets. The earliest is Alice Chapin's *At the Gates*. Reduced to one page for its 1909 publication in *The Vote*, the play offers us a suffragette posted at the exit gate of the House of Commons, where she waits throughout a cold and dreary night for any chance to distribute suffrage literature to MPs on their way home.[18] This woman, also generically named 'Suffragette', deals with both sympathetic and vicious responses from those around her.

The woman demonstrates her perseverance in making it through her long sentinel, even though she's been jailed for a similar posting in the past. She also demonstrates her rhetorical flexibility by working biblical parable, toughness, and elegance into her conversations. Nevertheless, one drunken man twice challenges her right to the streets with the question, 'Can you walk across Westminster Bridge at five o'clock in the morning?' She never answers him directly, but responds by noting her moral responsibility to campaign: 'Standing in the pillory is never pleasant. The one thing that makes me strong to endure is because I believe that I am working for the advancement of humanity.' The space of the streets is not necessarily desired by this woman, but she considers it her right and responsibility to be there and will fight fiercely to defend her 'territory'.

Two additional newspaper plays share in this attempt to re-imagine public space with women as full political participants. W. Pett Ridge's *A Good By-Election* takes place in a High Street at tea-time, as the political bustle surrounding a local by-election brings campaigning to the public square.[19] In a space that seems to resemble the rough and tumble of Hyde Park's Speakers' Corner, four voices vie for recognition. The three male voices offer hackneyed formulaic rhetoric of several kinds and the one female speaker stands apart as the most natural speaker. Though the crowd call out comments which attempt to make her public appearance a sexual prostitution ('Why don't you get a sweetheart?' and 'What about Kew Gardens next Sunday afternoon?'), she speaks ably on issues of women in prison and women's potential voting patterns. Her claim to space remains tenuous, however, since she has neither the last word nor crowd support.

Similarly in Lorimer Royston's *Fair Play*, a 'Modern Young Woman' takes part in a village bazaar after-tea discussion of votes for women.[20] As the 'Sleek Man' makes relentless charges against suffragists (and finds support from all but one of the other characters), the isolated Modern Young Woman rebuts the Sleek Man's comments with an impressive arsenal of facts. At one point the Sleek Man characterizes the Modern Young Woman's responses as 'guerilla warfare' to suggest that he needn't respond to her. Others dismiss her similarly.

I'd like to suggest that the suffragist characters in all four of these plays have indeed adopted 'guerilla' tactics, claiming space wherever they can with disregard to cultural precedent or personal danger. And as these women define both a new voice and a new space, they make determined, dangerous moves. Yet the characters display a curious mixture of passive/aggressive responses, and all four plays have a tentativeness uncharacteristic of suffrage drama. Claiming new spaces seems to be difficult. From the pages of suffrage newspapers, these plays (and others like them) offer a dramatic record of women's movement out of the Ibsenite drawing room. Simultaneously, they show how the women selling the newspapers full of such subversive theatre faced challenging situations. On the street as on the page, suffragists invaded new public spaces, unsettling the assumptions of those around them.

II The Suffrage Meeting: Performing Politics

In the study of suffrage theatre, it's dicey trying to draw the line between literary accomplishments and political ones. The plays I have discussed above are fictional literature, yet are enticing as an imaginative record of actual campaigning. In this second section, I would like to approach the indeterminate line between theatrical and political event from the other side, by examining some actual political events and their conscription of performance.

As suffragists called their forces together in both intimate and large-scale meetings, they relied on their knowledge of and their experience with theatre to shape the public face of the movement. Simply, I will argue that for these women to be political and claim space, theatre turned out to be their most reliable tool.

Let me begin by describing the 'Garden Fete' put on by the suburban Croydon Branch of the WFL one Saturday in the summer of 1912. Suffragists organized the event to raise money for the cause. What may be surprising is how at this late date in the campaign women were creating a public and political space modelled on familiar domestic concerns. The scene was 'cheerful, peaceful', with 'charming children', wives 'not cockpecked' and husbands 'not henpecked' who consumed 'excellent coffee, cakes, and ices'.[21] Homemade jams and sweets were also on sale and Mrs. Snow reportedly sold her hand-embroidered items at bargain prices.

Against this comfortable backdrop, the narrative thread of the event was provided by performance. After a speech by WFL President C. Despard and a programme of children's music, events were capped by the performance of Evelyn Glover's *A Chat with Mrs. Chicky* and Graham Moffat's *The Maid and the Magistrate*, two comic suffrage plays which clearly make the case for women's vote. The whole garden fete, then, may be seen as a performance which puts the audience in familiar woman-tended domestic space, only to remind them through actual plays that this homely feeling occurs in a public space newly accessible because of the movement toward enfranchisement.

This mixture of domestic comfort and propagandistic drama was present on a large scale also in the more public 'Yuletide Fest' of 11 December 1909, at the end of a year during which the campaign took on massive proportions: there had been protest marches, the London meeting of the International Suffrage Society, the first hunger strikes, and accelerating protest violence by suffragists.[22] Though much larger than the Croydon event (the Yuletide Festival took up the massive Albert Hall), it followed a similar pattern. The physical space was claimed through typically domestic paraphernalia (food and gift displays), crowned by the 'enormous Christmas Tree' from which President Despard and a 'Fairy Queen' distributed gifts to the children, the 'smaller suffragists'.[23] But the events of the day fill this comfortable space with demanding politics.

Mr. Israel Zangwill made sense of this move out of the domestic and into the public; he rallied those present by articulating their move away from the domestic space, 'anti-Suffrage was . . . an Idyll of domesticity – a poetry that too often forgot the prose facts. For woman no longer remained in her home; the industrial development took her from her hearth to spin by steam.'[24] Other prominent speakers joined Zangwill in calling for continued fortitude; and then, once more, events climaxed with theatre. Alice

Chapin's *At the Gates* was scheduled for performance, to commemorate 'the weary siege of Westminster this summer' ('Royal Albert Hall', p. 82), but was not performed, due to lack of time. However, four other plays (*The Pot and the Kettle*, *Press Cuttings*, *How the Vote Was Won*, and *Before Sunrise*) put on by the AFL had 'crowded houses' ('Yuletide Festival', p. 87); and the evening ended with the memorable staging of Cicely Hamilton and Edy Craig's *The Pageant of Women*:

There has never been anything like this Pageant, which brought the day to a fitting close. It sang in one's blood with its colour harmonies and the sonorous sound of its message.
('Yuletide Festival', p. 89)

Once more the Actresses' Franchise League (AFL) gave defining shape to a major political event, this time by making their dramatic art out of 'glittering propaganda'. Notably, the monumental sweep of *A Pageant of Women* shows how the suffrage street processions became a major component of the propagandistic plays women wrote. Indeed, this play threatens to march off of any stage as it displays its monumental parade of famous women (from Hypatia to Georges Sand, from St. Hilda to Joan of Arc, from Boadicea to Rosa Bonheur) to show women's cultural and political worth. With this performed at the close of a whole day's activities, the planners of the 'Yuletide Festival' effectively erase the line between political meeting and theatrical performance. The two are fused.

Though in a very different way, I would say the two are also fused in the most visible of all suffrage performances – the suffragists' massive marches through London. These marches are also perhaps the clearest signal that the suffragists were attuned to the scale of the cityscape in which they operated. The city is, as Elizabeth Grosz notes, 'the most immediate locus for the production and circulation of power'.[25] In their claims to power, the suffragists found themselves confronted specifically by the 'monumental spaces' of the city, places where those in a society mark their membership.[26]

Women felt, of course, that these male-inspired and directed spaces were meant to exclude them. Betsky articulates this exclusion with the example of the Champs-Élysées in Paris, when he writes of women's perennial exclusion from the boulevard, an over-sized, male-determined space. One might easily make a similar case concerning London's Trafalgar Square (a frequent location for suffrage rallies), dominated by the looming, out-of-scale, phallic Nelson's Column. However, in spite of such established, patriarchal mappings of London's public space, suffragists managed to claim a share of the monumental civic spaces of London for their own, again with theatre as their working model.

The Magnitude of the Marches

We must begin by remembering the magnitude of the public meetings and marches of the suffragists in London. The playwright Elizabeth Robins estimates that the WSPU held over 20,000 meetings from just 1909 to 1910, several times filling large venues like the Albert Hall, the Queen's Hall, and St. James's Hall.[27] The major marches which punctuated such a steady diet of meetings had even more impressive numbers. The early 'Mud March' of February 1907 saw over 3000 suffragists from forty organizations marching from Hyde Park Corner to Exeter Hall; and a year later, in June 1908, there were two huge marches.

First the NUWSS sponsored a two-mile march through London, the likes of which 'has never before been seen in London'.[28] Women from all over the country marched, representing local suffrage societies, international suffrage societies, professional and educational women, women union and guild members, and women writers. Ten to fifteen thousand women moved through the two-mile route to the Albert Hall. Commentators, remarking on the organizers' ability to bring together women of so many classes and creeds, were awestruck by the spectacle:

It was more stately and more splendid and more beautiful than any procession I ever saw. . . . The women have done what the men have failed to do. They have revived the pomp and glory of the procession.[29]

Amazingly, within another week, London was treated to a second, even larger demonstration, organized by the WSPU for 21 June 1908. Here, up to 30,000 women took seven different routes through London to converge on Hyde Park, blocking traffic all along the way. In Hyde Park, somewhere between a quarter- and a half-million people gathered. Photographs show a sea of supporters spread over huge open sections of the park: the protesters clearly claimed the monumental space of the park. Other processions followed in successive years, including the stately Women's Coronation Procession of 1911 and the grim 1913 funeral procession for suffrage martyr Emily Wilding Davison. But the very familiarity of the marches was such that strategists had to invent new themes and methods to maintain public (and media) attention.

While these events were newsworthy in their political novelty and constant innovation, it is the underlying conscription of theatrical structures and elements that most interests me. Indeed, such massive gatherings are usefully understood *as* dramas. The narrative line, for example, is always a variation of the same movement – large groups of women moving toward central London, staking a physical claim on the nerve-centre of public space. The characters in this drama of conquest are 'Suffragists' in multitudinous variation, women identified first and foremost by their politics, women willingly group-identified and stereotyped. The costuming is beautifully co-ordinated, with each organization adopting its own memorable set of colours (green and pink for the AFL; green, white, and gold for the WFL, purple, white, and green for the WSPU, etc). The props are carefully crafted banners which the women have designed and sewn, and now carry across the city as recognizable icons of freedom and political commitment.

And the sets, of course, are the monumental streets, parks, and squares of London. For, notably, these are dramas which make no pretence of rootedness in the home space. While suffragists' festivals and fetes draw from the domestic, these theatrical processions completely reject the confinement of interior space. In these memorable processions, women were improvising a new kind of political drama on the urban streets where political and cultural power is rooted.

Elizabeth Robins closes her account of the suffrage campaign with a geographical image in which militancy develops 'an explosive power which should crack the crust of ages'. She goes on to claim that in England the upheaval has been and will be dramatic: 'so have the deeps of the submerged sex been upborn to light, to the bright danger of the peaks, by those very forces which sought to hold her down' (p. 371). Her account highlights the triumphant mutability of women's public space in this period. As I now turn to analysis of more traditional theatre spaces, I hope to show how women's assumptions about theatre space alter along with these brazen public claims to space.

III New Theatre Space

When Ibsen's *A Doll's House* was revived at the Royal Court in 1911, M. Slieve McGowan urged suffragists to support a play whose advanced ideas were still all too rare: 'The Dolls' Houses of the world still, alas! are considered most desirable residences by a great number of both men and women.'[30] That the politicized women of London were still rallying their numbers to witness Nora's slamming of the home door suggests the uneven nature of their achievements in political, public as well as theatrical realms. Yet the unprecedented volume of plays written by women in the decade before the First World War is evidence of many women's commitment to joining Ibsen in the re-imagining of stage space.

Some of these plays are unabashedly political statements which call directly for the women's vote, from Elizabeth Robins's groundbreaking *Votes for Women* and Evelyn Glover's *A Chat with Mrs. Chicky*, to Isabel Tippett's *The Stuff that 'Eroes Are Made Of*. Other plays raised more general issues of women's rights and autonomy – dramas like Cicely Hamilton's *Diana of Dobson's*, Margaret Wynne Nevinson's *In the Workhouse*, and Bessie Hatton's *Before Sunrise*.

All the plays, however, reflect the altering of public and private spaces which was unavoidably central to the suffrage movement. While Millicent Fawcett and other moderate suffragists were at this late date still committed to a political life in which women would retain their rootedness in the home and be womanly women,[31] the majority of suffrage plays attack the traditional home as surely as the suffrage marches emptied them of women.

For example, H. Arncliffe Sennett, in *An Englishwoman's Home*, has the long-suffering heroine Mrs. Jenkins end the play acknowledging her home as a 'prison' from which she would like to flee.[32] In Edith Baker's *Our Happy Home*, an aunt, Belinda Verreker, and her niece, Sybil Egerton, must be coaxed by enlightened men to leave home for the cause. 'A woman's place is wherever there is work to be done and evils to be redressed', says Sir Joseph Wilmot.[33] And in *The Woman with the Pack*, this wandering figure inspires young Philippa to abandon domestic drudgery for probable arrest as a suffrage demonstrator.[34]

The Plays of Christopher St. John

The promise and peril of new spaces is also at the centre of the theatrical writing of Christopher St. John. I have chosen to focus on St. John for several reasons. First, she was involved in the theatricalizing of the suffrage campaign in major ways, from her feminist journalism (including theatre reviews) to her active campaigning to her multiple political plays. Second, and more uniquely, she came to her political commitment from two very different living spaces: first, central London flats in which she helped conceal suffragists on the run; and second, a remote cottage in the Kent countryside where she and her female domestic partners Edy Craig and Tony Atwood created a feminist pastoral retreat. The spatial range of her own life contributed, perhaps, to a dramatic *oeuvre* in which she cleverly and subtly challenged prevailing theatrical practice. Though not unique in her aesthetic innovations, her work includes some of the most sophisticated, influential, and politically astute of the many suffrage dramas.

St. John's two most performed plays were co-written with Cicely Hamilton, and both *The Pot and the Kettle* (1909) and *How the Vote Was Won* (1909) are comedies which argue for women's vote by making any other arrangement seem nonsensical. Like many suffrage plays, they offer conversion to the cause as their predictable narrative climax. I would like to pause over two slightly later plays, however – plays which demonstrate clearly how the processional quality of suffrage campaigning influenced this playwright's imagining of space.

The First Actress (1911) takes place in 1661, just after Margaret Hughes has finished a performance as Desdemona, taking an historic position as the first woman to perform on the London stage after the Restoration. Initially surrounded by men, she feels she's been made a fool, and is told women should not attempt acting, 'a sphere where she [woman] is totally unfitted to shine'.[35] The dismissive men soon abandon her, however, and as she sleeps Margaret is treated to a dream in which great actresses from the next 250 years visit to reassure her that her performance will be seen as the first of many stage triumphs for women.

The play becomes a pageant, then, as eleven famous actresses succeed one another in relating the future glories of women's stage presence; and this pageantry must have been enhanced at the play's initial performance when Edy Craig's Pioneer Players brought together many of the most noted actresses of the day to play these historical roles: Ellen Terry, Lily Brayton, May Whitty, Dorothy Minto, Lilian Braithwaite, Lena Ashwell, and others. Together with Craig's help, St. John was able to re-create on stage the linear space-busting processional pageantry that – in 1911 – would still have had the aura of gutsy protest. St. John's play is notable for its ability to bring on stage the spatial subversiveness of the street pageant.

In St. John's *The Coronation* (co-written with Charles Thursby) this same linear shaping of narrative and space dominates. Edy Craig and her Pioneer Players again produced the play, in which a nearly all-male cast works through a re-imagining of both political rights and social space. The play's satirical, political, and allegorical intentions are announced first in the naming of the characters, which range from Henricus XVI, King of Omnisterre, to Chief Minister Verbi-Verbi to Naval Lord Admiral Nihiltim.

The play takes place on the coronation day of King Henricus, whose role is designed to be only ceremonial, since Verbi-Verbi and his cohorts actually rule the country. As his coronation procession winds through the crowded city streets, however, the king has been horrified by the poverty he sees and distressed by one protester in particular:

Today at the corner of Cathedral Square one sufferer, braver than the rest – oh, sign of the times, it was a woman! – dashed through the soldiers with miraculous swiftness, miraculous courage, and threw this into my gilded coach![36]

She has delivered a paper with details of starvation, poverty, and despair. When she is found and brought to the king, she – the one who holds her head up high (p. 34) – offers him further specifics of her eighteen-hours-a-day working schedule, her son's death from starvation, and her vow to kill the king in revenge. She does attempt the murder, but the king's passivity stops her, and the two instead team up to force major social and political changes on the powers of Omnisterre – the coronation will be public for the first time, the king will sell his regalia to buy food for the poor, the House of Representatives to Parliament will be reconstituted, and universal suffrage will be proclaimed. Henricus says:

We shall abolish the arrogant judge-made interpretation of the word 'people'. In future, when we say 'people' in Omnisterre, we shall MEAN 'people', not 'men'. Women shall be citizens in the new Commonwealth!   (p. 49)

Like several other suffrage plays, this one is a political fantasy which imagines a radical solution to current ills. It stands out, however, because its solution is so vested in a political imagination which features massive numbers and political processions. Yet the very real threat this play posed may be measured in the handling it received from the Lord Chamberlain. While the play was performed on 28 January 1912 (again produced by Edy Craig and the Pioneer Players at the Savoy), the Lord Chamberlain's copy in the British Library is full of marks which signal his alarm at its politics, specifically its king and its critique of capitalism.

The political boldness of the piece may also be measured in its timing – the actual coronation of King George had taken place in June 1911, and the suffragists, of course, had marked the occasion with their own procession the Saturday before the event. With her play, however, which the International Suffrage Shop had published in 1911, St. John takes up the dark side of such a political changing of the guard.

'The Wilson Trial' and 'Her Will'

While such plays most obviously mark the ways in which the street campaigning of the suffragists altered theatre, I would like to turn finally to two plays, seemingly much more traditional, in which transformations of space may be more profound. In both, comedy and its focus on the future allow St. John to offer her most sophisticated proclamation on women's stage space.

The Wilson Trial was staged at the Court Theatre in 1909; here where Harley Granville Barker, George Bernard Shaw, and even Elizabeth Robins had so recently challenged the standards of contemporary drama, St. John offered the comic portrait of a young woman who turns a familiar domestic situation topsy-turvy.[37] Violet Trench, a 26-year-old Gaiety Girl, is called upon to rescue her wayward brother Edmund. She notes the 'comic' situation in which she's demeaned for playing 'the man' and is then needed to save her sibling from some damaging legal testimony.

Her knowing power is not so unusual in comedy; what is more notable is her worldly articulateness. And as she wrestles through the legal issues with Sir Leslie Roberts, her street wisdom is clear. Violet is not a suffragist, but her professional life on stage has educated her in the ways of the world. And because of that, she is able to turn her drawing-room space into a courtroom in which she betters the lawyer. He leaves saying, 'It is I who should thank you – you have taught me more in twenty minutes than I should have found out for myself in twenty years.' Violet has made the domestic space of her own sitting room a place for public negotiation and legal transaction.

Her Will, which St. John produced in 1914, is her most complete statement of this re-conceptualized interior space. While all the action takes place in the dining room of the recently deceased Helen Wilton, the coura-geous public life of suffragists determines dialogue, character interaction, and narrative. After the suffragists' years of campaigning, it's clear no one's home life can be the same. Helen Wilton has died from the health com-plications of being force-fed in Holloway Prison, having been jailed for suffrage demon-strations, and her funeral procession has celebrated the suffrage cause by replaying its distinguishing features.

'An occasion for a demonstration', the procession included twelve young girls 'wearing the colours of the Forward Suffrage Union' as pall-bearers and others donning gold sashes inscribed with 'Equalitas'.[38] Be-fore her death, Helen Wilton had been a major financial supporter of suffrage causes and, most significantly, the reading of her will during the play marks her continuing financial legacy to enfranchisement. She notes in the will that, while alive, 'I gave all I had to helping the suffrage army fight for the woman's cause' (p. 140). Now that she's dead, her remaining fortune is willed to the cause, until women win the vote.

While such a summary makes the play sound like a predictable political tract, it displays none of the dangerous public life of suffrage demonstrating; indeed, ironically, it is the counterpoint to this 'politically correct' behaviour and language which gives the play its theatrical life. For its action actually centres on the fates of Cicely and Raymond Wilton, their mother Mrs. Wilton, and Cicely's fiancé, Harry Vernon. It begins when Cicely, Harry, and Mrs. Wilton enter Helen Wilton's dining room to hear the will.

Cicely and her brother Raymond expect to inherit their aunt's fortune, but while the three await word of the specific bequests, they are assaulted by a domestic situation completely foreign (and distasteful) to them. Crocker, Helen Wilton's feisty maid, reminds them that she met Helen while the two were together in Holloway Prison. Crocker's life as an impoverished, abused woman con-vinced Helen to support Crocker and her children. As Crocker puts it, 'That's one good thing that's come of you ladies goin' to 'Ollo-way. You sees for yourselfes that some of us are there 'cos we never 'ad a chanst' (p. 3).

The three visitors show various signs of discombobulation at Crocker's aggressive presence, and then Raymond joins them, adding to the situation a full display of his pomposity. During this initial action, all four find ways of declaring their distaste for and distance from the suffrage cause and its disruptive public politics. When the lawyer arrives to read the will, however, they find themselves irretrievably implicated in the suffrage cause. Cicely and Raymond remain potential inheritors, as it turns out; they will receive what's left of Helen Wilton's fortune when the women's vote is won.

As Helen has apparently 'willed', this thrusting of the cause into the centre of their lives brings on immediate ideological reposi-tionings. Raymond blames his mother and sister for critiquing suffragists publicly: 'It's a great pity all the same Cicely that you and mother used to talk so openly against Woman's Suffrage' (p. 16). Cicely and Harry see their marriage plans dissolve at this deferring of her inheritance. She bemoans her enforced idleness – 'I wish to God I hadn't been brought up to be perfectly useless' (p. 17) – and he feels forced to defend his: 'I have been encouraged to be idle on Cis's expectations ever since we became engaged' (p. 18).

At this nadir of their recognitions, Miss Loring-Parke, the suffragist left to super-intend Helen Wilton's fortune for the cause, enters and shows them all how her politics of equality could be in their best interest. Not surprisingly, her gracious common sense wins the day. Harry hints at his own conversion,

Mrs. Wilton affirms social connections with Miss Loring-Parke's family, and the play ends with these non-suffragists creeping comically to political conversion. The play is confined to the domestic space of a dining room and all public campaigning remains off-stage, yet St. John has managed to create a play in which domestic space no longer represents confinement for women, and serves instead as a location for political conversion and female autonomy.

St. John's play is representative of many suffrage dramas which similarly reconfigure women's space. A woman's home is no longer a place of psychic battering, angst, and re-crimination. This is because sometimes the home actually is *hers*, and as a result it has become the launching pad for assaults on public space as well as a resting space where women regroup

New Space for Suffrage-ing Women

When Elizabeth Robins spoke to suffrage supporters gathered in the Albert Hall in March 1912, she rallied support with her image of 'the wandering spirit of militancy' (p. 308); she cited campaigners' new-found ability to sprout wings (p. 307) and to be unbound by particular locations, be they jail, home, or country. This may overstate the power of the suffrage campaign's ability to transform physical space; but in its extreme, her image marks persistent efforts to redraw public perceptions of women's relations to place and space. Motivated by their fierce political battle, women made theatre a central model for claiming both agency and space. So whether we date the phenomenon at 1910, 1906 or 1914, we should remember the British women who saw so clearly that performance could liberate space as well as minds.

Notes and References

1. 'The Pioneer Players', *Common Cause*, 15 June 1911, p. 178. The actress Ellen Terry's conversion of Shakespearean heroines into suffrage leaders is the specific subject-matter in this review.

2. Elizabeth Wilson, *The Sphinx in the City: Urban Life, the Control of Disorder, and Women* (Berkeley: University of California Press, 1991), p. 14.

3. See Woolf's essay 'Character in Fiction', in *The Essays of Virginia Woolf, Vol. 3, 1919–1924*, ed. Andrew McNeillie (New York: Harcourt Brace Jovanovich, 1988), p. 421. Henri Lefebvre echoes Woolf's sentiment in his study of social space, noting that: 'The fact is that around 1910 a certain space was shattered. It was the space of common sense, of knowledge (*savoir*), of social practice, of political power, a space hitherto enshrined in everyday discourse.' He elaborates later on the specific role of painters in this change: 'Around 1910 academic painters were still painting "beautiful" figures in an "expressive" way: faces that were moving because they expressed emotions. . . . The pictorial avant-garde, meanwhile, were busily detaching the meaningful from the expressive. . . . If we are to believe the most authoritative commentators, the turning-point was 1907.' See *The Production of Space*, trans. Donald Nicholson-Smith (Oxford: Blackwell, 1991), p. 25, 300-301.

4. Hanna Scolnicov, *Woman's Theatrical Space* (Cambridge: Cambridge University Press, 1994), p. 7

5. Una Chaudhuri, *Staging Place: the Geography of Modern Drama* (Ann Arbor: University of Michigan Press, 1995), p. 55.

6. Aaron Betsky, *Building Sex: Men, Women, Architecture, and the Construction of Sexuality* (New York: William Morrow, 1995), p. 139.

7. Dolores Hayden also notes how attempts to limit women's freedom have been instrumental in defining both public and private space: 'One of the consistent ways to limit the economic and political rights of groups has been to constrain social reproduction by limiting access to space. For women, the body, the home, and the street have all been arenas of conflict.' Dolores Hayden, *The Power of Place: Urban Landscapes as Public History* (Cambridge, Mass.: MIT Press, 1995), p. 22.

8. Lorraine Code, *Rhetorical Spaces: Essays on Gendered Locations* (New York: Routledge, 1995), p. xiii.

9. As reported in 'Other Suffrage News: The Actresses' Franchise League', *The Vote*, 23 December 1909, p. 105.

10. 'Selling the Paper', *The Common Cause*, 17 March 1910, p. 690.

11. C. Despard, 'The Vote: an Appeal', *The Vote*, 19 December 1913, p. 130.

12. Ethel Fennings, 'Selling *The Vote*', *The Vote*, 14 January 1911, p. 141.

13. F. W. P. L., 'Getting New Readers', *Votes for Women*, 27 January 1911, p. 270.

14. 'Votes for Women Fellowship', *Votes for Women*, 14 February 1913, p. 287.

15. 'Paper-Selling Report: an Original Christmas Procession', *Votes for Women*, 12 December 1913, p. 163.

16. 'An Idea for a Summer Holiday', *Votes for Women*, 28 May 1909, p. 724.

17. Gladys Mendl (Mrs. Harrie Schutze), '*Su' L' Pavé*: Being Half an Hour in the Life of a Paper-Seller', *Votes for Women*, 9 January 1914, p. 224.

18. A. Chapin, *At the Gates*, *The Vote*, 16 December 1909, p. 94. The full play is in the Lord Chamberlain's Plays at the British Library. It was scheduled for performance on 13 December 1909 at the Albert Hall. The play was not performed, however, due to an over-full bill at the Albert Hall that night. See 'Secretary's Report, June 1909–1910', AFL Archives, Fawcett Library, p. 6.

19. W. Pett Ridge, *A Good By-Election*, *Votes for Women*, 8 April 1910, p. 441.

20. Lorimer Royston, *Fair Play: a Dialogue*, *Votes for Women*, 13 February 1914, p. 298.

21. All details of the fete come from E. M. N. C., 'At Play – with a Purpose – at Croydon', *The Vote*, 13 July 1912, p. 209.

22. It was one of several such large-scale events; the WSPU had sponsored the 'Woman's Exhibition' in May.

23. 'Royal Albert Hall. – Yuletide Festival', *The Vote*, 9 December 1909, p. 82.

24. E. T., 'Yuletide Festival', *The Vote*, 16 December 1909, p. 87.

25. Elizabeth Grosz, *Space, Time, and Perversion: Essays on the Politics of Bodies* (New York; London: Routledge, 1995), p. 109, 105.

26. Lefebvre makes this point that 'monumental space' is a location where those in a society mark their membership (op. cit., p. 220).

27. Elizabeth Robins, *Way Stations* (New York: Dodd, Mead, 1913), p. 196.

28. *Morning Leader*, 15 June 1908, as quoted in Lisa Tickner, *The Spectacle of Women: Imagery of the Suffrage Campaign, 1907–1914* (Chicago: University of Chicago Press, 1988), p. 88.

29. James Douglas, *Morning Leader*, 14 June 1908, as quoted in Tickner, op. cit., p. 88.

30. M. Slieve McGowan, 'Ibsen at the Court Theatre', *The Vote*, 18 March 1911, p. 254.

31. See Fawcett's earlier speech, 'Home and Politics: an Address Delivered at Toynbee Hall and Elsewhere' (London: Central and East of England Society for Women's Suffrage, *c.* 1887).

32. H. Arncliffe-Sennett, *An Englishwoman's Home*, (1910), in *Sketches from the Actresses' Franchise League*, ed. Viv Gardner (Nottingham Drama Texts, 1985), p. 20.

33. Edith M. Baker, *Our Happy Home*, *The Vote*, 30 December 1911, p. 115–17.

34. Gertrude Vaughan, *The Woman with the Pack*, *Votes for Women*, 22 December 1911, p. 187.

35. Christopher St. John, *The First Actress*, 1911, Lord Chamberlain's Plays, British Library.

36. Christopher St. John and Charles Thursby, *The Coronation* (London: International Suffrage Shop, 1911), p. 30.

37. Christopher St. John, *The Wilson Trial*, 1909, Lord Chamberlain's Plays, British Library. Edy Craig was the producer for the one matinee performance.

38. Christopher St. John, *Her Will*, 1914, Lord Chamberlain's Plays, British Library.

Susan Oommen

Inventing Narratives, Arousing Audiences: the Plays of Mahesh Dattani

In this article Susan Oommen looks at the plays of the popular Indian dramatist Mahesh Dattani as conversations between the writer and his audience on models of reality, and interprets their performance as moments in subjectivization. In initiating an audience into redefining identity, she argues that Dattani provides the parameters within which problematizations may be reviewed and better understood. He also seeks to queer the debate on Indian middle-class morality, thereby challenging its privileged status and underscoring the interconnection between repression and invisibility. The question for the audience is whether Dattani's plays can cue them into experiences of resistance and encourage them to reinvent narratives that may then function as personal histories. One of the plays on which this article focuses, *Dance Like a Man*, was seen during this year's Edinburgh Festival as part of the Celebration of Indian Contemporary Performing Arts. Susan Oommen works in the English Department in Stella Maris College, India, where she has been on the faculty since 1975. She spent the past academic year at the Institute for Research on Women at Rutgers University.

MAHESH DATTANI'S plays talk to the audience. Sometimes they call for recontextualization of response; sometimes they suggest revisioning in what may appear to be standard cultural discourse. Dattani's conversations raise questions from recent years, questions that pertain to power and gender. What is the thinking that allows exploitation to happen? Who selects the narrative that is to be written out of history? When do differences become pathological? What is the historical process that validates exclusion as first principle? These cumulate into the overarching question about how to make sense of identity.

Dattani, who has come into his own as an Indian popular playwright, is seen today as a pragmatic writer who has the capacity to deal with obsessive issues head-on. His audience, in the main, is drawn from the ever-growing, English-speaking Indian middle class which has come to form a metropolitan fraternity. Audiences emerge from performances of *Dance Like a Man* (1989), *Final Solutions* (1993), and *Seven Steps Around the Fire* (1999) excited about their contemporaneity. For some, however, there is a sense of unease that in performance there may have been an oversimplification of vocabulary. It is almost as if the audience has been brought under scrutiny.

What protocols of reading will they subscribe to? In the problematization of morality, how will they process the narrative? Will they segregate the story or make it their own? Dattani's observation in his preface to *Collected Plays* (2000) seems to take a swing at this process: 'I have yet to meet a homosexual who says, "I have nothing against heterosexuals, but do we have to watch them on stage?"'[1] The comment, even as it critiques the concept of a collective middle-class audience, serves to queer both audience sensibility and identity, unpacking the collective as multiple bodies with distinct histories and oddities, inhabitants of separate territories, yet participants in civil society. Dattani seems to be throwing more than the symbolic challenge to reciprocal identity[2] in the overt suggestion that respect for ambivalence is tied into respect for freedoms.

Indian society has evolved over the years, as any living organism must, from closed traditional settings to open, forward looking environments, marked by movements, collective action, awareness of exclusions, the

Mahesh Dattani, born in Bangalore on 7 August 1958, studied in Baldwin's High School and St Joseph's College of Arts and Science, Bangalore. He has worked as a copywriter in an advertising firm and subsequently with his father in the family business. His theatre group Playpen was formed in 1984, and he has directed several plays for them, ranging from classical Greek to contemporary works. In 1986, he wrote his first full-length play, *Where There's a Will*, and from 1995 he has been working full-time in theatre. In 1998, he set up his own theatre studio dedicated to training and showcasing new talents in acting, directing, and stage writing, the first in India to focus specifically on new works.

In 1998, Dattani won the Sahitya Akademi award for his volume of plays *Final Solutions and Other Plays* (East-West Books, Chennai), thus becoming the first English-language playwright to win the award.

Dattani teaches theatre courses at the summer sessions programme of Portland State University, Oregon, USA, and conducts workshops regularly at his studio and elsewhere. He also writes plays for BBC Radio 4.

Photo: Dattani with actress Lillete Dubey during rehearsals of *Dance Like a Man*.

Dattani initiates his audience into the politics of lack in the area of identity. A dead father's mistress ridicules a son's pretensions to self-determination. A dancer becomes displaced when his self-esteem is brutalized. A surviving Siamese twin refashions the past for meaning. The sense of lack explodes in *Final Solutions*. A wrought-up chorus intones: 'What must we do? To become more acceptable? Must we lose our identity? O what a curse it is to be less in number' (p. 208).

Dattani would have his audience believe that the politics of lack is also the politics of being the minority in India. How does the non-heterosexual stake out his territory and demystify the gaze of the heterosexual custodian of truth? How does the non-majority negotiate, when the majority holds control? 'You can have an angry mob outside your house. You can play the civilized host. Because you know you have peace hidden inside your armpit' (*Final Solutions*, p. 192).

Dattani never baits his audience, though. His plays provide the spatial and temporal parameters within which problematizations may be reviewed. On stage he uses memory, provides physical spaces for both past and present, locates separate actions at multiple levels, transforms faces into masks, frenzy into voices, within contexts that are only too familiar. *One Muggy Night in Mumbai* (1998) can bring into the living room where the action in the play is located all at the same time the Mumbai skyline and the beauty and the terror it can hold for those who are shut out, the bedroom where the worst manipulations can happen, and the mainstream daylight world, at once buoyant, inquisition-ridden, and destructive. The playwright's offer to the audience is the insight into contrasting structures in identity.

The Narrative on Sexuality

One Muggy Night in Mumbai explores fear, loathing, and helplessness, closing in on confrontation: the moment of coming out.

BUNNY: All I am saying is that we should all forget about categorizing people as gay or straight or bi or whatever, and let them do what they want to do!

need for alternative codes, and the interrelation between the personal and the public. Areas of conflict, however, contend in the discourse (or its lack) between rationalized systems and alternative experiences.

RANJIT: Well, I am sorry. There is such a thing as honesty. Or maybe it is the company you keep. Or maybe it is the country I am in.

BUNNY: Why don't you go back to England or wherever if you are ashamed to be here?

RANJIT: Buggery do! I will be where I want to be, thank you.

BUNNY: You can leave the country, but you can never run away from being brown. You are ashamed of being Indian.

RANJIT: That's really rich coming from a closet homosexual like you! Yes, I am sometimes regretful of being an Indian, because I can't seem to be both Indian and gay. But you are simply ashamed. All this sham is to cover up your shame.

BUNNY (*really hurt*): That's not true. You cannot make me an outcaste both inside and out.

DEEPALI: Bunny, you are a Sardarji. Why did you cut your hair?

BUNNY: What has that got to do with it . . . ? Okay. Not because I am ashamed of being a Sardar. I am proud of it. I believe in my faith. My children learn from the Guru Granth Sahib . . . But because if I had a turban, I will end up playing a stereotypical Sird in all those movies. And that would hurt even more.

DEEPALI: Thank you, Bunny. I rest my case, Ranjit.

RANJIT: What do you mean?

DEEPALI: It's not shame, is it? With us? It's fear. Of the corners we will be pushed into where we don't want to be. (p. 89)

One Muggy Night in Mumbai

The fear of becoming the stereotype presumably lowers resistance to muscle-flexing and returns the subject to the closet. For the custodian this is a time-tested strategy in violence that will allow him or her the moral sanction to locate sexuality within parameters of heterosexuality. In the play Kamlesh and Prakash break up because Prakash knows Kamlesh still loves Sharad, who plans to marry Kiran, Kamlesh's sister, in the hope that the marriage will provide him the cover to return to his relationship with Kamlesh.

Ridiculous as it may seem, this set-up underscores the reality of contemporary India. The arrangement is picked up in *Bravely Fought the Queen* (1991), and Dattani offers a further variation in *Do the Needful* (1997), in which Lata and Alpesh enter into a marriage contract in order to allow each other the freedom to pursue their separate lives – Lata with Salim, Alpesh with Trilok. The nexus between compulsory heterosexuality and discursive categories[3] and the essentialist stance that sexuality is subject to mechanisms of repression[4] seem to inform, one more time, the narrative on sexuality in India.

Muggy Night throws up two worlds with two separate geographies. One of the two worlds carries the larger space because it has assumed the power to exclude. The smaller world may be seen in the circle of friends who have come together at Kamlesh's apartment; the larger world lies outside, celebrating the ritual of marriage. The mood inside is hardly festive – in fact everybody feels betrayed at some level. Just as Kiran begins to understand her brother's world, she sees a photograph of her brother and his lover, in the nude. She recognizes the lover as her fiancé Ed, whom her brother had always affectionately called Prakash. She is devastated. Ed works himself into a fury. He tries to jump off the ledge. The friends save him: 'You will survive, Ed. Come back in!' (p. 109). He hits Kamlesh and hurls insults from the straight world: 'Faggot! Pansy! Gandu! Gandu!' (p. 110). Weeping, he turns to Kiran: 'I am sorry. . . . I didn't mean to harm you. I only wanted to live' (p. 110).

Patterns of Camouflage and Survival

Dattani's audience, themselves perhaps strangers to Article 377 of the Indian Constitution outlawing same-sex relationships,[5] may find themselves increasingly preoccupied with patterns of camouflage and survival. Two particulars begin to work on the audience's memory: the recurring reality of herpes, and the option of death in a world without exits. Herpes, with its post-seventies sexual association, requires no decoding. When Sharad points out to Kamlesh that he can never forget Prakash because he will keep cropping up like herpes (p. 58), the audience has already entered a discourse on normative sexual behaviour. Death as an option is a little more uncomfortable to deal with in a world that offers hotlines for help. It is not the first time that Ed has contemplated killing himself, only because he is not sure if there is anybody who wants to hear his story. And every time someone has listened to his story, and held his hand, and looked at the trees, and told him they were beautiful together, even if the larger world could not see him, he has deferred death.

Herpes perceived as shame and death perceived as cleansing serve to highlight the homophobic psychiatrist who is present in the play, who is present in Amnesty reports, and who is present in the collective audience too. The diagnosis is illness, the remedy reorientation. Kamlesh confesses that he had traced feelings of shame directly to his psychiatrist: 'I wished I wasn't gay' (p. 69). He gets rid of both his psychiatrist and his fear. Bunny believes that one must follow basic animal instinct and camouflage in order to blend with the surroundings; Sharad asserts, 'Honey, if you flaunt it, you've got it'; Kamlesh wants to make peace with himself: 'I don't want to flaunt or hide anything' (p. 70).

Eventually the argument falls back onto the audience. Kiran clarifies the position, as it were: 'If there are any stereotypes around here, they are you and me. Because we don't know any better, do we? We just don't know what else to be' (p. 107). In her recognition that she is what she is by default, Kiran is as much victim as anybody else in the play. But what becomes her saving grace is her willingness to acknowledge realities that lie beyond borders and probably beyond grasp too.

In *Final Solutions* Dattani locates bigotry as critical to both loss of memory and political violence. At the heart of *Final Solutions* lies the parable of the boy-hero who was forced into a choice that took away from him the myth of the hero.

> A minor incident changed all that. There may have been others which Javed didn't talk about. I can't remember how it started. Oh, yes. There was the cricket match. Not much of a match. We were playing cricket on our street with the younger boys. The postman delivered our neighbour's mail. He dropped one of the letters. He was in a hurry and asked Javed to hand the letter over to the owner. Javed took the letter . . . and opened the gate. Immediately a voice boomed, 'What do you want?' I can still remember Javed holding out the letter and mumbling something, his usual firmness vanishing in a second. 'Leave it on the wall,' the voice ordered. Javed backed away, really frightened. We all watched as the man came out with a cloth in his hand. He wiped the

Mahesh Dattani fields a question from the audience at a discussion following the performance of *Dance Like a Man* at the Portland International Performance Festival. Also present: Michael Griggs, the artistic director of the festival, along with the actors, Lillete Dubey, Suchitra Pillai, Joy Sengupta and Vijay Crishna.

letter before picking it up, he then wiped the spot on the wall the letter was lying on and he wiped the gate! We stared at him as he went back inside. The postman came out of the next house and grinned when he saw this. 'Take no notice,' he said. 'That man is slightly cracked.' We all heard a prayer bell, ringing continuously. Not loud. But distinct. The neighbour had been praying for quite a while, but none of us had noticed the bell before. We'd heard the bell so often every day of our lives that it didn't mean anything. It was a part of the sounds of the wind and the birds and the tongas. It didn't mean anything. You don't single out such things and hear them, isolated from the rest of the din. But at that moment . . . we all heard only the bell.

Pause. Quietly, in a matter-of-fact manner.

The next day, the neighbour came out screaming on the streets. Yelling at our windows. We peeped out. He was furious, tears running down his face. We couldn't understand a word he was saying. I found out later. Someone had dropped pieces of meat and bones into his back yard. . . .
I didn't speak to Javed for many days after that. I was frightened of him. For months, whenever we played cricket and heard the bell, we remembered that incident and we avoided looking at Javed. And for Javed, he was – in his own eyes – no longer the neighbourhood hero.   (p. 200–1)

The rest of the play builds on versions of this tale. Anger, pain, sacrilege, repudiation, denial, and shame go into spin. Muslim *versus* Hindu, minority *versus* majority, defiance *versus* authority.

The crux of the play is the political fallout that results from the murder of a temple priest and the collapsing of space between the personal and the public. In the momentum that builds, the near-impossibility of returning to the boy-hero or of looking at the self away from superstructural encoding become all too real. The plot plays out until the audience begins to worry. Did the post-Ayodhya riots[6] happen before or after the play? Was Dattani analyzing possibilities, or was he chronicling history, or was he looking at demons?

Separate Communities, Separate Worlds

The fear of being pushed into corners and the strategies of survival and of appropriating spaces that Dattani explores in *Muggy Night* come to haunt the worlds of Ramnik, Smita, Javed, and Bobby in *Final Solutions*. Nightmares unfold in the recognition that separate communities must inhabit separate worlds. There is no room for personal space. The mob takes over. The only community marker that the mob as chorus wears is a mask; other factors are common – victims and aggressors, helpless and oppressive. *Final Solutions* may be about people running from each other. It may also be about the scent that drives the pack. The play tracks the relentless search for the scapegoat. The direction begins to turn inward: what it is that must be excluded from history to gloss the demonizing of the self. Dattani stylizes this brutality in the mentality of a riot-mob.

The Chorus pounds with their sticks.

CHORUS ALL: Why won't you open the door?

JAVED (*pleadingly to Ramnik*): Please don't. We beg of you.

CHORUS ALL: Open up! Or we'll break your door!

RAMNIK: No!

Spotlight on Ramnik. The Hindu Chorus strike more stylized positions on top of the ramp and speak from within their masks.

RAMNIK: What harm have they done to you?

CHORUS 1: Set an example.

CHORUS ALL: Stop them.

CHORUS 1: Before they do harm.

CHORUS ALL: Tame them.

CHORUS 1: Before their passions inflame.

CHORUS ALL: Thwart them. So we may live in peace.

RAMNIK: We?

CHORUS ALL: We, who are right.

RAMNIK: And they?

CHORUS ALL: They who are wrong. Since we are right. And they oppose us. (p. 181)

Ramnik must prove he is the liberal Hindu. Javed understands that Ramnik hates him simply because he has proved Ramnik otherwise. Smita must display righteous indignation even if she betrays the trust her friend Tasneem has placed in her, in confiding the family secret that her brother Javed is a jihad-mercenary, hired to start riots, to be the one 'to throw the first stone' (p. 195). Bobby is ashamed of who he is and camouflages the Muslim name Babban. Just as Bobby tries to turn Javed away from the violence of mind-

less rioting, Smita's outburst works against him. Bobby returns the audience to the fable. He picks up the Hindu idol to prove to Javed the absurdity of imaginary sacrilege and the senselessness of payback:

> You can bathe Him day and night, you can splash holy waters on Him but you cannot remove my touch from His form. You cannot remove my smell with sandal paste and attars and fragrant flowers because it belongs to a human being who believes, and tolerates, and respects what other human beings believe. That is the strongest fragrance in the world.
>
> (p. 224–5)

Final Solutions troubles the audience with a question from the past, of the sense of belonging, of strictures of inclusion and exclusion.

In an exercise that seeks to queer the debate on consensus and socio-cultural unity, Steven Seidman expresses reservations about the moral vision of a rational society associated with the Enlightenment. He observes:

> At issue is the question of whether today it is still credible and desirable to invoke an ideal of a unified humanity, of a transcendent truth, a strong notion of cultural consensus, and the very idea of social progress.[7]

The debate pertains to differences and the human being's ability or inability to enter into reconfigurations. Paulo Freire adds a fierce political twist to this speculation on epistemology in the equation:

> If, then, marginality is not by choice, marginal man has been expelled from and kept outside of the social system and is therefore the object of violence.[8]

The leap of faith for the middle-class Indian, if the audience is to go by *Final Solutions*, has been in the direction of violation.

Disability as Alternative Experience

For Dattani there seems nothing sacrosanct about any point of view, because at any given time it may only be one among several points of view. In *Tara*, Dattani posits the freak against the non-freak. On the one hand is the world shared by Chandan and Tara, the conjoined twins consigned to medical history, one-legged and sterile, clever, intelligent, witty, but apprehensive about the external world. Tara comments: 'Two lives and one body, in one comfortable womb. Till we were forced out' (p. 324).

On the other hand is the world of Bharathi and Patel, Dr Thakkar, Roopa – inheritors of the world of normality, myopic, selfish, cruel, and surrounding themselves with protective rules. Access to the world belongs to them. Alone after the death of Tara, Chandan relocates to London as Dan. But Tara's death haunts him; it is as if he has had no personal history at all. That their mother made a politically incorrect choice in Chandan over Tara, in the matter of apportioning a limb, does not make matters easy. He hopes to find salvation in writing. He acknowledges that if he must feel, he must open the flood-gates of memory, and create personal history, even if it means appropriating Tara's tragedy.

Patel and Bharathi live out unforgiving lives, unrelenting in both their inability to forgive themselves and their cruelty to each other. Consumed by guilt and indignation, not only do they fail to create the spaces their children require for growth, but they also dehumanize the limited spaces they are given access to. The method of stunting in the art of growing *bonsai* that Dattani uses as a metaphor in *Bravely Fought the Queen* seems to apply to the freaks of the world. Chandan's comment at the end of the play – 'Those who survive are those who do not defy the gravity of others. And those who defy even a moment of freedom, find themselves hurled into space, doomed to crash with some unknown force' (p. 379) – hints at the odds stacked against anyone who does not have the cover of cultural consensus.

Presumably the audience is not forced into corners because *Tara* seems to be about the human heart and about choices and decisions that allow the human being to approach disability as alternative experience. But at the primary level *Tara* initiates the audience to a world without the protective rules of resemblance and causality. It suggests that chaos may be a condition that rational thinking cannot keep at bay, or even

Dance Like a Man

Bravely Fought the Queen

that the rules of normality may have to be redrawn. It posits that environments may be altered, providing the impetus for opening up which, in philosophy, someone like Deleuze would explain as a constant loss of ideas – which indeed is a normal process, because 'thinking takes place in the relationship of territory and earth'.[9]

Deleuze's argument seeks to view earth as embracing elements together, rather than as one among other elements, in its capacity to use these elements to 'deterritorialize territory'. Dattani seems very gently but very definitely to be overriding boundary markers. Devoid of markers, social constructs lose legitimacy. *Tara* comes to pose the fundamental question: who creates the freak?

The Invisible Minority

In what seems to be a recurrent pattern, Dattani creates a bipolar world in *Seven Steps Around the Fire*. The point of reference is marriage. The world of the *hijras*, the freak community who cannot procreate, and the normal heterosexual community who necessarily must procreate, form this bipolarity. *Seven Steps* has all the makings of a thriller. The murder of Kamala, a *hijra*, unravels as an act of homophobia. It is an execution carried out by a father to protect his son. The case is closed. Two factors seem to account for the silencing: one, that the father carries political clout; two, that homophobia may be indulged. Sharma has his son Subbu's bride Kamala murdered, because to him it is unthinkable that his son can be gay. He seeks to force his son into a heterosexual wedding, the Hindu ceremony in which the groom holds his bride by the hand and takes the ritualistic seven steps around the fire. As Sharma claims, 'My truth is in ensuring he is on the right path' (p. 37). The ritual doesn't quite work. Subbu kills himself. Echoes from *Muggy Night* sing in:

KIRAN: I really wish they would allow gay people to marry.

RANJIT: Oh, they do. Only not to the same sex.

(p. 98)

Uma Rao, who does research on *hijras*, sees herself as a sociologist turned sleuth. She meets with the *hijras*. Her intentions are good. The community wishes her well, gives her a charmed locket that assures her mother-

hood, but pleads that she leave them alone. There can be no interaction between the two worlds. To the fanatic, 'one *hijra* less in this world does not matter' (p. 35); the refrain goes, 'Back! Beat it! Kick the *hijra*!' (p. 7). For the *hijras* life goes on unnoticed by the other world. Uma explains:

> The invisible minority. Behind Russel Market, everyone knew where to find them, although I couldn't see any *hijras* on the streets. They only come out in groups and make their presence felt by their peculiar loud hand clap.
> (p. 21–2)

The only instance when the groups accord mutual visibility is at marriage and birth, when the majority group sanctions the minority group the power to bless through their singing and dancing and clapping. In the event of infertility, the *hijra* becomes the scapegoat: a lack of blessing is cited. Uma comments on the irony:

> The two events in mainstream Hindu culture where their presence is acceptable – marriage and birth – ironically are the very same privileges denied to them by man and nature. Not for them the seven rounds witnessed by the fire god, eternally binding man and woman in matrimony, or the blessings of 'May you be the mother of a hundred sons.'
> (p. 11)

Indian middle-class morality presumably defines its core in the principle of polarity, and the basic assumption that it requires a saint to create a sinner and *vice versa*. Having assigned all subscribers particular places in the grand scheme, the moral custodian cannot account for non-categorized elements which, when they do surface, follow convention, maintaining semblances of contiguity. The convention however brings undue pressure on persons or groups falling outside the grid.

Dattani showcases the venerated Indian family in *Bravely Fought the Queen* and *Dance Like a Man*. The Indian joint family is introduced in costume: the mother-in-law, two sons married to sisters, the brother-in-law, also a close friend, and the family business. Behind the mask lies whoring, wife-beating, pretence of marriage, either because of the absence of love or because the husband is gay, forbidden embraces in strong, dark arms, mistresses, shady business deals.

Bravely Fought the Queen carries the ironic Indian middle-class line: 'The best part about the ball is everyone will be in costume! And we will have masks on!' (p. 237). The plot uncovers two figures: the saint and the sinner. The saint is Praful, who threatens to burn his sister when she is seen with a boy-friend. The saint arranges for his sister to marry his lover. The saint burns his lover with guilt and shame because they are not heterosexual. And Ed goes through similar motions in *Muggy Night*. The sinner is Alka, the sister who can never have a husband because the saint is her husband's lover. For her there is no end of the road because she remains in costume. She learns to be content with simple-minded distractions: drinking, enjoying the sensual music of Naina Devi, and wild dancing in the rain. Her sigh, 'Aren't there times when you don't know what you are doing?' (p. 300) is as close as she gets to answers.

Dattani continues to map Indian morality as cruel and repressive in *Dance Like a Man*, where he presents the unhappy history of a passionate young dancer who is stripped of desire and self-esteem. In a plot conceived by his father and abetted by his dancer-wife, he is rescued and sacrificed because his father believes 'a woman in a man's world may be considered as being progressive. But a man in a woman's world is pathetic' (p. 427). His marriage collapses, his infant son dies from an overdose of opium, his career fails to take off, and he wallows in drunken cynicism: 'We were only human. We lacked the grace. We lacked the brilliance. We lacked the magic to dance like God' (p. 447).

Dattani appears to be extremely sensitive to the sense of defeat in cynicism which, the way he comes to see it in *Final Solutions*, leads to procrastination and the point of no return:

HARDIKA: Do you think . . . do you think those boys will ever come back?

RAMNIK: If you call them they will come. But then again – if it's too late – if they may not come.

The lights fade out slowly and go off last on the men standing amidst the Mob/Chorus and their masks.

(p. 226)

Dattani's plays help audiences to cue into experiences of resistance, opening windows on how separate worlds come to be constructed. He seems to work on a certain assumption that his audience may be willing to go with him. In the distancing that under-scores much of the parody in his plays, he seems to encourage his audience to invoke events and characters who exist off-stage. The post-orientalist Indian familiar with the argument of his colonized ancestor that non-Europeans were also capable of rational thinking, presumably recognizes not only the non-necessity to reduce distinctness but also the necessity to avoid distortions. Any audience which begins to look at officially designated spaces as politically tenuous may apprehend agency as political prerogative.[10]

The Preoccupation with Identity

Dattani makes no claim to be creating epic theatre; neither do his critics. But Sharad's voyeuristic comment in *Muggy Night* – 'Oh, my Gawd! Those heterosexuals are at it again!' (p. 53) – or Anarkali's inability in *Seven Steps* to consider Uma as sister because Uma is not a *hijra* (p. 13) draw on audience recognition that these are parodies of hege-monic behavioural patterns. In addition the audience is also keenly aware of the male/female identity of the actors playing the *hijras*.

In a note on fluidity of identities, Butler explains the sense of perpetual displacement that drag or cross-dressing brings about in performance. She argues that the 'parodic proliferation deprives hegemonic culture and its critics of the claim to naturalized or essentialist gender identities', and creates a climate for resignification and recontextual-ization.[11] The kind of popularity Dattani enjoys, because it evokes an extremely easy relationship between playwright and audi-ence, makes the passage possible. In fact the audience may even be willing to consider the performance as a moment in subjectivization, evolving out of conversations between audience and variation models of reality. To challenge privileged status and thereby to problematize it[12] becomes one more option in an evening of performance.

In positing fable as a counter to the-end-of-the-world, Lyotard writes:

Rigid systems like a bent bow or even an instinctual programme (to borrow examples from living things we know) prohibit amoebas, sycamores, or eels from fabling, as a general rule.[13]

Substitute eels *et al.* for the 'other', and Paul Monette's statement reads like an affidavit: 'Genocide is still the national sport of straight men, especially in this century of nightmares.' And he continues, 'Why do they hate us? Why do they fear us? Why do they want us invincible?'[14]

This correlation, as it were, between repression and invisibility may be sourced in a lack of discourse. Grand narratives and monologues create implosions, while distinct narratives presumably generate multiple readings. Separate narratives make a seemingly strong case for geographical spaces – community, nation, metropolis – into which future people may enter. Dattani seems to be suggesting to his audience different ways of seeing spaces: hanging upside down from a tamarind tree, cutting down the tree, or just reinventing other ways of seeing the world (*Where There's a Will*, 1988).

In Dattani, contemporary audiences recognize the magic of individuation. But this time the actor becomes located in the audience rather than on stage. Instead of recognizing the private person behind the actor's mask, the audience glimpses the separate men and women behind the mask of the middle-class audience. Subtexts come into their own. The preoccupation with identity continues. In riding the wave of redefinition, identities come to territorialize or deterritorialize or renegotiate or altogether reinvent environments.

The commercial bent, the parody, the middle-class down-to-reality thinking, and the story-telling make it possible for straight,

linear audiences to enter the world of fabling which has already made spaces for amoebas, sycamores, and eels. There they imagine and recreate subtexts in which they may be both actor and playwright, listening to and inventing narratives that would belong to both individual and community, and which begin to act out as personal histories.

Notes and References

1. Mahesh Dattani, *Collected Plays* (New Delhi: Penguin, 2000), p. xi-xii. All citations from Dattani are from this edition.

2. Alberto Melucci, *Nomads of the Present: Social Movements and Individual Needs in Contemporary Society* (Philadelphia: Temple University, 1989), p. 129. Melucci locates absence of reciprocal identity – 'I recognize myself and I am recognized/I recognize myself and I recognize the other' – as a consequence of breakdown in interaction, caused by suffering such as marginality or stigmatization.

3. Judith Butler, *Gender Trouble: Feminism and the Subversion of Identity* (New York: Routledge, 1999), p. 24.

4. Michel Foucault, *The Use of Pleasure*, trans. Robert Hurley (New York: Vintage, 1990), p. 4.

5. *Breaking the Silence: Human Rights Violations Based on Sexual Orientation* (New York: Amnesty International, 1994), p. 38. Article 377 of the Indian Constitution criminalizes sexual behaviour between consenting adults of the same sex.

6. In 1992 militant Hindu activists, aspiring to construct a Ram temple, wrecked the Babri Masjid in Ayodhya. Communal riots were orchestrated directly afterwards.

7. Steven Seidman, *Difference Troubles: Queering Social Theory and Sexual Politics* (Cambridge: Cambridge University Press, 1997), p. 1.

8. Paulo Freire, *The Politics of Education: Culture, Power, and Liberation*, trans. Donaldo Macedo (Massachusetts: Bergin and Garvey, 1985), p. 48.

9. Gilles Deleuze and Felix Guattari, *What is Philosophy*, trans. Hugh Tomlinson and Graham Burcell (New York: Columbia University Press, 1994), p. 85.

10. Judith Butler, 'Contingent Foundations: Feminism and the Question of "Postmodernism",' in *Feminism and Methodology: Social Science Issues*, ed. Sandra Harding (Bloomington: Indiana University Press, 1987), p. 47.

11. Judith Butler, *Gender Trouble*, p. 175.

12. Stevi Jackson, 'Heterosexuality, Power, and Pleasure', in *Feminism and Sexuality: a Reader*, ed. Stevi Jackson and Sue Scott (New York: Columbia University Press, 1996), p. 175.

13. Jean-Francois Lyotard, *Postmodern Fables*, trans. Georges Van Den Abbeele (Minneapolis: Minnesota University Press, 1997), p. 94.

14. Paul Monette, *Becoming a Man: Half a Life Story* (London: Harcourt Brace Jovanovich, 1992), p. 2.

Michael David Fox

'There's Our Catastrophe': Empathy, Sacrifice, and the Staging of Suffering in Beckett's Theatre

In his seminal *The Theatre of the Absurd*, Martin Esslin suggested that Samuel Beckett, in denying his characters individualized facets of humanity, achieved an 'alienation effect' that was more profound and assured than Brecht's. Here, Michael David Fox, while agreeing that Beckett denies actors and audiences the kinds of identification achieved in naturalistic drama through Stanislavskian techniques, argues that he demands a different quality of empathy from his audiences – not through the artifice of a character's simulated pain but through the actuality of the performer's physical suffering. While analyzing the demands and constraints upon actors which Beckett imposes in his better-known plays, he also re-evaluates the more 'occasional' piece *Catastrophe* – written in 1982 ostensibly as a homage to the then-imprisoned Czech playwright Vaclav Havel – less as a critique of political terror than as an ironic and devastating self-critique of the terror of Beckett's own tragic representation. Michael David Fox is a doctoral student in drama and critical theory in the Joint Doctoral Program in Drama at the University of California, Irvine and the University of California, San Diego. His dissertation is on the production of empathy in Shakespeare's tragedies. He wishes to thank Robert Weimann, Wolfgang Iser, and Gabriele Schwab for their helpful and generous comments on earlier drafts of this essay.

TODAY the theatre in the West, as practised over at least the last three hundred years, is confronted with a host of cultural changes that are more radical and challenging than it has ever before experienced. The growing impact of new technologies of body-free mass communication, the declining authority of writing and written texts, the emergence of hypertext, and the increasing global inter-action and exchange of cultural goods have only just begun to affect the theatre's tradi-tional practice of scripted performances in shared, bodied spaces.

While it is certainly too early either to forecast or fathom the resulting transform-ations in the theatre in their full extent and direction, the new cultural and theoretical investments in 'performance' and 'perform-ativity' may point the way. The concepts of 'performance' and 'performativity', as well as related concepts such as 'theatricality', 'play', 'stage', and 'spectacle', continue to en-croach upon linguistic and semiotic models as the primary matrix for the analysis and critique of an exceptionally broad range of cultural products and processes, including literature, politics, psychology, gender, and race.

Given the fact that these essentially theat-rical concepts have already achieved the momentum to serve as the next paradigm across the humanities, it is striking that in this conjunction the theatre itself has been largely by-passed by the recent cultural energies that have drastically expanded and privileged both the practice and theory of 'performance'. Yet since so much is now at stake across so many disciplines in under-standing the parameters and meaning of performance, we ought not to neglect to do so in what we might call, at least in regard to western culture, performance's natural habitat, the theatre.

The by-now notorious gap between the expansion of the performance paradigm and drama in production is marked by the absence in the recent debate of any serious consideration of the most crucially conditioning factor of contemporary theatrical performance – the rise of disembodied, virtual spaces, and corresponding changes in audience reception, expectation, and response. The shared, bodied space of the theatre may be 'incommensurable', to use Jean-François Lyotard's term, with the new bodiless mass technologies and their social/cultural needs.[1] On the other hand, the shared, bodied space of the theatre can perhaps serve as a unique and relatively accessible site of resistance to what Fredric Jameson has called 'the waning of affect in postmodern culture'.[2]

'Am I as much as . . . being seen?'[3]

The present essay is both deeply concerned with and conditioned by this state of affairs. Pursuing further the crisis of representation in the postmodern culture, the essay addresses widely underestimated and specifically theatrical uses of bodied space in the performance of the plays of Samuel Beckett. Paying special attention to areas of what Judith Butler cites as the 'incongruity' and 'inseparability' between speech and body,[4] I shall explore Beckett's uses of bodied performance space for creating powerful affective relationships between performers and spectators.

As I will show, Beckett's plays in performance create spaces where performers' bodies, over and beyond the perception of performed ones (i.e., beyond the imaginary figurations called 'characters'), directly and powerfully affect the spectators. Beckett's theatre thus enlists what Pierre Bourdieu has called the 'practical belief' of the body: 'The body believes in what it plays at: it weeps if it mimes grief.'[5] Pointing well beyond both the Brechtian anxiety about identity poetics and the Stanislavskian obsession with psychological realism and the closure of representation, the bodied space of Beckett's theatrical performance can be shown to provide both diminishing representations and new openings for empathy.[6]

When Beckett's theatre works were first staged, even the most admiring and insightful critics believed that his recondite, spectral characters foreclosed the possibility of audience identification or empathy. Martin Esslin, for example, wrote in 1961 that the 'Theatre of the Absurd', including Beckett, achieved a greater 'alienation effect' than Brecht because:

with such characters it is almost impossible to identify; the more mysterious their action and their nature, the less human the characters become, the more difficult it is to be carried away into seeing the world from their point of view.[7]

For Esslin, the incomprehensibility of the actions and motives of Beckett's figures prevents such identification and forces the audience to view them with 'a cold, critical, unidentified eye' that precludes empathy.[8] But Beckett's theatre incites more than the cold intellectual fire of the mind; the heart is profoundly engaged, anguished, and even restored by the characters who inhabit Beckett's disfigured landscapes of absence.

What triggers the spectators' profound emotional response to Beckett's spectral figures? This essay argues that the source of the empathy and deep affective response elicited by Beckett's theatre is, in large part, the result of the audience's awareness of the presence and very real suffering of the Beckett actor. Beckett's theatre forces the actor to suffer and the audience to perceive the reality of that suffering. The anguish that Beckett's plays appear to stage as the represented suffering of fictional figures is in fact existentially present in actors on stage: empathy in Beckett's theatre is created by staging of anguish's presence, not its representation, in the body and soul of the actor.

As Esslin's comment reveals, traditional performance theory is inadequate to explain the production of empathetic response by Beckett's theatre; its failure to account for the emotional density of Beckett's plays points towards a radically different understanding of how theatre produces empathetic response in the audience. Beckett's dramaturgy refutes the traditional conception of the relationship between the production of empathy and the conventions of illusionistic theatrical representation.

In particular, the dynamics of affective response to Beckett's theatre discredit the relationship traditionally believed to exist between the production of empathy and naturalistic acting, including a rejection of traditional assumptions about affective response and the performance of 'character'. In sharp contrast to what traditional performance theory would lead us to expect, Beckett's theatre creates and increases the spectators' empathetic engagement through a dramaturgical strategy that subverts representation and ensures the audience's acute awareness of the actor's presence.

'Me – to play'[9]

Performance theory has traditionally linked the production of empathy in the theatre to the audience's ability to invest greater psychological reality in the theatrical character than in the living, present actor. It is through this process of theatrical illusion that the actor is transformed from a commonplace existence into the majestic fiction of the enacted role. According to traditional dramatic theory, this kind of illusionistic or representational performance is necessary for the creation of audience empathy with the fate of theatre's fictional characters. As Esslin put it, it is necessary that the audience identify with the fictional subjectivity of the characters and be 'carried away into seeing the world from their point of view'.[10]

It is also axiomatic for traditional performance theory that the production of empathy requires the performance to achieve, as completely as possible, the disappearance of the subjectivity and presence of the representing actor into the fictional subjectivity of the represented character. Since empathy is thought to be contingent on belief in and identification with the fictional subjectivity of the characters, the spectator's awareness of the existential presence of the actors' own subjectivity must be overcome; actors must not be seen nor heard in their own human particularity and presence, but disappear into the theatrical image of fictional characters.

Performance theory has assumed that for empathy to be produced, this same process

of spectatorship must take place in the theatre. The representing actor must disappear into the represented character to the same extent that Jacques Derrida has described the disappearance of the linguistic signifier into the praxis of language: 'The graphic image is not seen; and the acoustic image is not heard.'[11] In the same way, in the theatre of mimetic representation the human beings who are representing actors are neither seen nor heard in their own human particularity and presence, but disappear into the mode of the theatrical image in the process of representation.

The source of the belief that representational illusion is necessary for the empathic response of the audience can be traced back at least as far as Denis Diderot's 1757 call for a theatre of total illusion, in which the spectators' awareness of the representing elements, particularly the body and psyche of the actor, is completely displaced by awareness of the representation.[12] As Diderot urged, the progression in acting style in the course of the next century was towards an ever more 'natural' or 'realistic' acting style, in which actors strove to conceal 'the fictitious nature of their representation' – that is, to conceal their concrete reality and presence behind the illusion of their roles.

The success of the imperative toward representational verisimilitude was so complete that by the time of the great modernist playwrights such as Ibsen, Shaw, Chekhov, and O'Neill, it became inconceivable that acting could be anything *but* an attempt at presence's disappearance into absolute representation. The dramaturgy of these playwrights contributed to the disappearance of the actor's presence, since the theatre they created was fundamentally a theatre of text in the form of representational dialogue. As Peter Szondi explains in *Theory of the Modern Drama*, the drama of modernity is therefore characterized by the 'absolute dominance of dialogue'.[13] For the dialogue of the great modernist playwrights was assiduously crafted to create the illusion of non-theatrical speech, since, as Szondi further observes, the modern theatre's demand for illusionistic dialogue and representational verisimilitude permitted no space for the spectator's awareness of the existential presence of the representing actor within the fiction of the represented role.[14]

The acting theory of modern drama also supported the belief that for an empathetic response to be produced in the audience, the actor must completely disappear into the illusion of character. The founder of modern actor training, Constantine Stanislavski, developed an acting theory aimed at getting 'from an actor a living, organic embodiment on the stage, to get the feeling that in the scene there are not actors but living people'.[15] To achieve this aim, Stanislavski sought 'a complete merging of the actor with the role',[16] so that both the audience's awareness of the actor and also the actor's awareness of the audience completely disappears.

Stanislavski's acting theory rested on the belief, shared by most theatre artists and theorists before and since (including those, like Brecht, who were opposed to Stanislavski on other grounds), that the production of empathy is dependent on the audience's ability to invest greater psychological reality in the theatrical character than in the living, present actor. Thus, following Stanislavski, Robert Cohen, in his widely used introductory college textbook on theatre, teaches students that there is a necessary correlation between the production of empathy and the conventions of fourth-wall realism, which Cohen calls 'indirect performance':

Indirect performance, however, is probably the more fundamental mode in drama; it is certainly the one that makes drama 'dramatic' as opposed to simply 'theatrical'. For indirect performance is the mode whereby the audience watches interactions that are staged as if no audience were present at all. As a result the audience is encouraged to concentrate on the events that are being staged, not on their presentation. In other words, the members of the audience 'believe in' the play and allow themselves to forget that the characters are really actors and that the apparently spontaneous events taking place before their eyes are really a series of scripted scenes. This belief . . . engenders audience participation *via* the psychological mechanism of *empathy*. In other words, the audience is likely to feel kinship with certain (or all) of the characters. . . . When that happens, the audience experiences the 'magic' of the theatre.[17]

Bruce Wilshire also offers an exemplary statement of this belief. There are, Wilshire states, in the theatre:

moments in which in which *our awareness of the actor is so peripheral*, and at the same time so confident and secure, that we can 'let go' and identify profoundly with the character he or she is acting. These are moments in which unprecedented extensions of our sympathy can occur, or in which regressions to archaic identifications and fusions with others can transpire. . . . The catharsis of one's emotions of pity and fear . . . is *possible only because one has identified with a person who is nevertheless fictional*.[18]

Since the goal of most theatre performance was and is to create these moments in which 'unprecedented extensions of our sympathy can occur, or in which regressions to archaic identifications and fusions with others can transpire', theatre practice following Stanislavski sought to suppress the spectator's awareness of the body and presence of the performing actor.[19]

Bertolt Brecht, despite his political and aesthetic differences with Stanislavski, agreed that Stanislavski's representational approach to acting 'systematically compels the empathy of the spectator'.[20] For Brecht, this belief meant that representation had to be exposed as illusion in order to prevent the spectator from experiencing empathy with the fate of the characters. Brecht's rejection of empathy was grounded in his conviction that the spectator's empathy with the illusory suffering of theatrical characters is a kind of 'witchcraft' that produces 'intoxication' instead of thought.[21]

To combat empathy, Brecht advocated an 'alienation effect' (*Verfremdungseffekt*) utilizing non-representational devices which included direct audience address, songs, placards, and narration, as 'an alternative to the empathetic response evoked by traditional pity and terror'.[22] The alienation effect 'was intended to "estrange" or "distance" the spectator' from the characters and the fictional event, and thus to 'prevent empathy and identification with the situation and the characters and allow the adoption of a critical attitude toward the play'.[23]

According to Brecht, the destruction of representational illusion would prevent empathy by making the audience aware of the theatrical medium itself, including, crucially, an awareness of the separation between the actor and the role. Despite his own repeated failures to foreclose empathetic response to figures such as Mother Courage through anti-representational techniques, Brecht did not question the equation of empathy with representational illusion. Following Brecht, contemporary performance theory, even the most anti-representational, has not questioned the dogma that representational illusion is necessary for empathetic response.

'If only I were not obliged to manifest'[24]

Contrary to the expectations and assumptions of traditional dramatic theory (whether allied with Stanislavski or Brecht), Beckett's plays create and increase the spectators' empathy by subverting the representational process. Even the most representational theatre contains an eradicable residue of the existential reality of the performance's own time, place, and means of production. As Robert Weimann has explained, 'this residue is the act of performance itself, at least insofar as it involves an irrepresentable energy, labour, needs, and exhaustion of the actors' minds and bodies'.[25] The existential presence of the actor/image in the theatre creates a potential disruption of the spectator's transference of reality from the signifying to the signified.

The representational theatre necessarily operates within a schemata in which 'what is cancelled, however, remains in view'.[26] The human substratum of the representing actor, unlike the graphic, acoustic, or filmic image, remains within the performance at least as a spectre, ever partially in view, and always retains the possibility of fully reclaiming an individual existence apart and distinct from the theatrical image. It is precisely this eradicable possibility of a face-to-face situation that defines the existential confrontation between the spectator and actor in the theatre: the actor on stage can never be subsumed entirely and irreversibly by the represented image.

The theatre, therefore, can never become simply an art of representation, since the actor's subjectivity is never wholly subsumed by the performance and the actor always possesses the potential to disrupt the illusion of a referent outside and apart from the actor's own performance. When, as in Beckett's plays (or Brecht's or Shakespeare's), the theatre purposely calls attention to its fictionality and the fact of performance, the actor's presence is thrust even more forcefully into the spectator's consciousness; the audience is directed to become conscious, in Robert Weimann's phrase, 'not of what is represented . . . but of what was representing and who was performing'.[27]

Beckett's characters continually point to the artifice, conventions, and apparatus of the theatre, and to their own status as theatrical entities. In *Waiting for Godot*, for example, Didi and Gogo simultaneously stage and comment on a music-hall routine:

VLADIMIR: Charming evening we're having.

ESTRAGON: Unforgettable.

VLADIMIR: And it's not over.

ESTRAGON: Apparently not.

VLADIMIR: It's only the beginning.

ESTRAGON: It's awful.

VLADIMIR: Worse than the pantomime.

ESTRAGON: The circus.

VLADIMIR: The music-hall.

ESTRAGON: The circus.

The self-consciously theatrical repertoire in *Godot* also includes Estragon's deadpan sarcasm as he peers into the auditorium ('Charming spot . . . Inspiring prospects . . . Let's go.'), Pozzo's 'lyrical' soliloquy on the weather, Lucky's dance, the Marx Brothers-like business of the exchanging of hats, Vladimir's song ('A dog came in the kitchen/And stole a crust of bread . . . '), ironic half-asides to the audience –

VLADIMIR: This is becoming really insignificant.

ESTRAGON: Not enough.

– and Estragon's topping epithet 'Crritic!'

Endgame goes even further than *Godot* in staging self-conscious performance in Clov's Buster Keaton pantomime with the ladders, Hamm's 'Me – to play', Clov and Hamm's actorly asides about the play they are performing –

HAMM: This is deadly . . .
CLOV: Things are livening up . . .
CLOV: The end is terrific!

– and Hamm's sardonic comments on turning the telescope on the audience: 'I see . . . a multitude . . . in transports . . . of joy. (*Pause.*) That's what I call a magnifier.' As Wolfgang Iser has pointed out, there is a 'loss of representation' achieved in *Endgame*, so that the spectators 'continuously run up against the resistance of an incomprehensible "reality".'[28]

In *Godot*, *Endgame*, and other Beckett plays, the actor does not so much engage in mimetic representation as subvert representation by *exhibiting performance*. The actor in Beckett's theatre presents, not represents. As Joseph Chaikin has explained, the actor in Beckett's theatre is

a performer doing vaudeville for the audience. The audience is in the theatre, the performer is on stage; this is a reality of the theatre. The actor, as performer, entertains the audience by doing routines.[29]

For Brecht, this subversion of the representational process is intended to produce in the spectators an 'attitude of detachment'.[30] To ensure such a response, Brecht insisted that his actors adopt a narrative style of acting, in which the audience is made aware of the difference between the detachment of the actor and the *agon* of the character. In contrast, in Beckett's theatre the subversion of representational illusion is not permitted to result in any consistently detached or objective response through the strategy of constructing the *mise en scène* so that the existential reality of the actors' performance replicates the agonized condition of his stage figures. Both Brecht and Beckett lead the audience away from perception of fictional, represented events, and toward perception of the existentially present actor, but while

Brecht leads the audience to awareness of the actor's detachment, Beckett leads the audience to an awareness of the actor's suffering. The Brechtian actor *demonstrates* the character's situation; the Beckettian actor *undergoes* and *suffers* it.

Martin Esslin has asserted that the emotional power of Beckett's plays is a product of his 'visual poetry' and the 'overall impact of a single overwhelming powerful image'.[31] But Beckett's visual poetry and powerful images are not staged without a severe price paid by the actor, whose body and soul must create the anguished shapes and sounds demanded by Beckett's vision. To appropriate a line from Beckett's *Watt*, the effect of Beckett's work on the actors who make the commitment to perform them is 'to saddle [the actor] with meaning, and a formula, so that [the actor] could neither think of them, nor speak of them, but only *suffer* them'.[32]

Actress Billie Whitelaw states that when Beckett directs, 'I will turn myself inside out, and I have made myself ill, trying to complete the image he has in his mind's eye and in his ear.'[33] Beckett does not allow the actor merely to simulate or represent suffering; the conditions of performance in a Beckett play ensure that the actor's suffering is real. Beckett constructs his *mise en scène* so that the position of the actors on stage is existentially the same as that of the characters they represent. As a result, the suffering that the audience sees and feels in a Beckett play is not primarily represented or illusionary; it is real and existentially present before the audience. As Beckett has insisted to his actors, 'Don't act, for God's sake.'[34]

Joseph Chaikin agrees: in performing in Beckett's plays, 'there is a level where the actor, *as a person*, is talking to each of the people in the audience, as a person, on that level where each is absolutely and completely alone'.[35] Here is the probable source of Beckett's reputation, reported by Beckett biographer James Knowlson, of not being an 'actor's director'.[36] Knowlson quotes Brenda Bruce, who played Winnie in the first London production of *Happy Days*, as recounting that she asked Beckett during rehearsals 'Do you want some acting to go on? And I'm not sure that he really did, you see.'[37]

Rather than indicating, as Knowlson supposes,[38] lack of understanding of the actor's creative process, Beckett's attitude reflects his careful construction of his plays so that *acting is not necessary*. In Beckett's theatre, acting, in the sense of a psychological process of imaginatively adopting a fictional character's motives and intentions, would be a hindrance to empathetic performance, since it would interfere with both the actor's experience of undergoing the existential situation of the performance inscribed in the *mise en scène* and the spectator's direct perception of the actor's presence.

For this reason, Beckett as a director did not allow the actors to 'work through' their roles through internal techniques such as improvisation.[39] As the German actor Klaus Herm, who performed in *Godot*, *That Time*, *Play*, and *Ghost Trio* under Beckett's direction, has affirmed, in Beckett's theatre there is 'nothing there to improvise'.[40] Similarly, Beckett as a director spent little or no time discussing with his actors psychological motivations or the naturalistic backgrounds of the characters.[41] Beckett insisted instead on exactitude and minute precision in the actor's embodiment of the role's physical elements, such as gesture, intonation, and rhythm.[42]

Walter Asmus, who was Beckett's assistant director for the majority of his German productions, reports that in rehearsals with the actress Hildegard Schmahl for the Berlin production of *Footfalls*, 'I can't remember any real motivation which Beckett gave . . . about why she should speak her lines in a certain way.'[43] Instead, Beckett concentrated on showing the actress the 'position of the body'. Asmus relates that:

Beckett used to stand with his arms crossed like this [*he assumes the posture of May*], looking forward, pacing, and seeing things with his mind. And what he said was very forceful, very sharp then. And that has to do with the position of the body. If you grip your arms and you have a fixed, physical point here where you hold yourself together more or less, you can speak rather easily and sharp at the same time without pushing it with the body. . . . It's a technical thing, which of course doesn't give the actress any inner motivation. . . . How do you explain to an actress why to speak it this way, which he gives as a line-reading? He didn't really give any reasons for that.[44]

Here, too, is the probable basis for Beckett's repeated requests that his actors play their roles without emotion.[45] As his notes to Peter Hall's London premiere of *Waiting for Godot* show, Beckett was not opposed to emotion in his plays. On the contrary, Beckett gave Hall numerous instructions calling for more extreme and detailed emotion from the actors.[46] Beckett's most frequent comment to Hall regarding what he wanted from the actors' performance was: 'More anguished.'[47]

In his later plays, Beckett did direct his actors to refrain from creating emotion. The reason for the difference between Beckett's approach to the acting of *Godot* and his later plays is his recognition that the *mise en scène* of *Godot* did not constrain and control the actors as did his later plays. *Godot* did not place the actor in the same existential condition as the characters, and so required from the actors both interpretation and representation. After *Godot*, Beckett's theatre did not need to generate emotion through *mimesis* or imagination. *Real* emotion, in the form of physical and psychological suffering, comes to the actor as a result of carrying out the instructions precisely set forth in the text. Emotion created through the actor's artifice would get in the way.

From *Endgame* on, Beckett thus ensured that there would be no question of needing interpretation or representation; henceforth, Beckett ensured that emotion in his theatre would not be generated by acting, but by 'the power of the text to claw',[48] and to claw the actor first of all.

'I can't go on, I'll go on'[49]

To perform in a Beckett play is to undergo and endure physical pain which is nearly always intense and which can be excruciating. H. Porter Abbot has described 'what Beckett does to his actors':

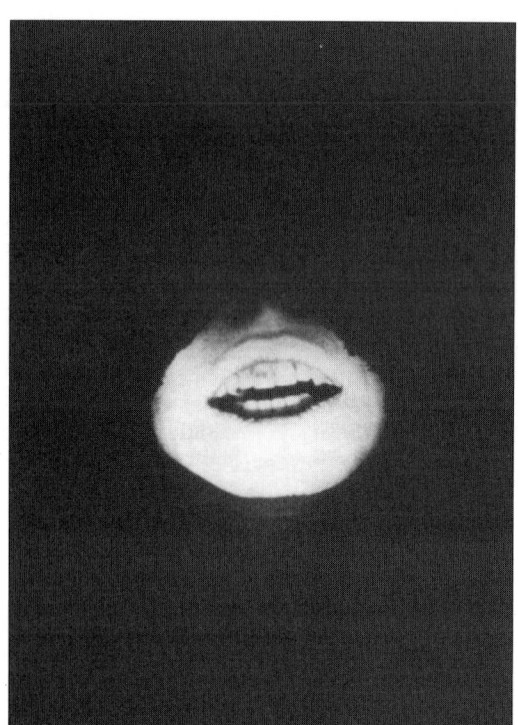

Above: Billie Whitelaw as Mouth in Beckett's *Not I*
(Royal Court, 1973). Opposite page: Alan Webb as
Willie and Peggy Ashcroft as Winnie in Peter Hall's
National Theatre production of *Happy Days* (1977).

'up to above her waist',[55] and in *Play* the actors are enclosed in urns about one yard high, 'the neck held fast in the urn's mouth'.[56] The actor playing *Krapp's Last Tape* must endure a 'laborious walk' throughout the performance,[57] the actors in *Quad* must perform their seemingly endless geometric courses as 'unbroken movement' and 'without rupture of rhythm.'[58]

The breakneck speed of utterance that Beckett often insisted upon could also cause physical pain for the actor. Knowlson reports that in rehearsal for the London production of *Play*, 'the actors were astonished at the speed at which they were being urged to deliver their lines', while 'Beckett argued that the lines should be delivered even faster'.[59] And Klaus Herm reports that in performing *That Time* (*Damals*) under Beckett's direction,

there was always the technical difficulty of speaking without breathing. . . . Beckett didn't want any pauses except for the three specified in the text. Without period or pauses, and as much as possible without breathing![60]

The human body in Beckett's texts is constrained, deformed, mutilated, and mutated, yet continues to offer resistance. In *Molloy*, the narrator speaks of using his mangled and crippled body as a weapon against the engulfing viscidity of the earth:

With time, and nothing but my teeth and nails, I would rage up from the bowels of the earth to its crust, knowing full well I had nothing to gain. And when I had no more teeth, no more nails, I would dig through the rock with my bones.[61]

The body is also figured as the concrete, material ballast that prevents Beckett's characters from decisive movement, weighing them to the spot, preventing any impulse toward an end of consciousness. As Gabriele Schwab has observed, the narrator of *The Unnamable* finds it 'impossible to sever himself from the notion of a concrete body'.[62]

The body for Beckett is at once a beginning and an end ('Astride of a grave and a difficult birth . . . the grave-digger puts on the forceps') and also that which prevents the ending. In *Endgame*, *Play*, *Happy Days*,

He ties ropes around their necks and crams them into urns. He ties them to rockers. He buries them in sand under hot blinding lights and gives them impossible scripts to read at breakneck speed. The word for this is torture.[50]

Billie Whitelaw has recounted Beckett's reaction after seeing her bound down with straps and braces for a performance of *Not I*: '"Oh Billie", Beckett cried, when he gazed upon his immobilized creature, "what have I done to you".'[51] The physical aspect of the 'torture' endured by the Beckett actor is the inscription of the character's physical situation on the actor's body. Joseph Chaikin recounts that while acting the role of Hamm in *Endgame* his impressions 'are those of a blind man: playing Hamm, I cannot see, but I can hear and feel the quality of the room'.[52] The actor playing Clov must endure the length of *Endgame* with a 'stiff, staggering walk',[53] the actors playing Nag and Nell must squat in ashbins,[54] the actress playing Winnie in *Happy Days* is encased in a mound

and *Rockaby* the body is the means by which consciousness is shackled to the endless anguish of existence. Crucially, in Beckett's theatre, the suffering produced by the physical constraints, deformations, and mutations of his figures are not *represented* by the actors; they are staged in the *existential reality* of the actors' bodies.

The emotional and spiritual conditions of Beckett's theatrical figures are also staged rather than represented in the existential reality of the actors' psyches and souls. Even more onerous than the physical torments of Beckettian performance are the psychological and spiritual demands that Beckett's plays make on the actor. The emotional and spiritual weight of the plays are enough in themselves to take a heavy toll on the actors: as Beckett wrote in *The Lost Ones*, 'The effect of this climate on the soul is not to be underestimated.'[63]

Irene Worth relates that in performing *Happy Days*, she 'had to go to a special doctor, because I'd got into a terrible muscular spasm through tension'.[64] Billie Whitelaw, who has performed in *Play*, *Happy Days*, *Footfalls*, *Rockaby*, *Enough*, and *Not I*, relates that acting in Beckett's plays is 'far more difficult, exhausting, and emotionally draining than doing twelve hours a day of *The Greeks* at the Royal Shakespeare Company. . . . [Beckett's] short pieces are like all of that condensed into an hour.'[65] Whitelaw finds that Beckett's plays 'are an absolute powerhouse of emotion',[66] while Eileen Blumenthal reports that 'each time Chaikin has become immersed in Beckett's work, he has come to feel drained by it – and then angry at having been lured into a world that saps rather than restores energy. He has said during these periods that he "hate[s] Beckett".'[67] As actor Alvin Epstein has remarked, for an actor in Beckett's plays, 'the grief is real'.[68]

The condition of suffering, merging the physical and the psychological, that Beckett has returned to most consistently is what

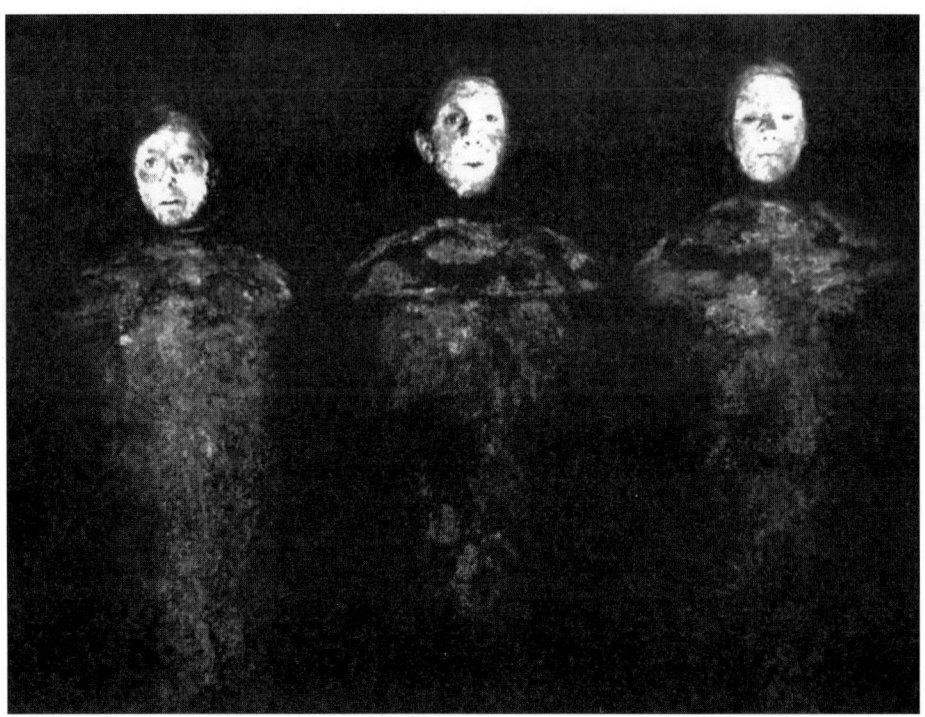

Beckett has called the 'anguish' and 'agony of perceivedness'.[69] For Beckett's figures, pierced by blazing light or entombed by murk and shadow, *essi est percipi* is a malediction. In *Not I, Cascando, That Time, Rockaby,* and *Ohio Impromptu*, Beckett dramatizes this agony of perceivedness by placing a silent, auditing (perceiving, audience) figure on stage along with the speaking (performer) figures. In *Play*, Beckett stages 'the agony of perceivedness' by placing three figures on stage whose speech is 'provoked by a spotlight projected on [their] faces'.[70] The spotlight acts as a mute 'inquisitor', a silent and archetypal Other,

> Just looking. At my face. On and Off . . .
> Looking for something. In my face. Some
> truth. In my eyes. Not even . . . Mere eye. No
> mind. Opening and shutting on me . . .[71]

The actors are compelled to 'face undeviatingly front throughout the play.'[72] The 'agony of perceivedness' in *Play* is not represented by the actors, it is undergone by them. The actors in *Play* are positioned in relation to the audience in the same manner as the characters are positioned in relation to the spotlight: seen, and judged, by silent, invisible inquisitors, who may or may not be paying any attention. The same situation holds in other Beckett plays. In *Happy Days*, for example, the actress playing Winnie is compelled to face into 'blazing light'.[73]

In Beckett's texts, the agony of being seen is paralleled by the anguish of *not* being seen, of 'something gone wrong with the silence'.[74] *Play* also stages the unresolvable ambiguity of the agony of perceivedness: The figure designated 'W2' says to the light: 'Are you listening to me? Is anyone listening to me? Is anyone looking at me? Is anyone bothering about me at all?'[75] Or as 'M' repeats twice at the close of the play: 'Am I as much as . . . being seen?'[76] This ambiguity of fear of being/not being seen is also expressed in Winnie's continual questioning of whether Willie can hear her,[77] and in Estragon's question in *Waiting for Godot*: 'Do you think God sees me?'[78]

Perhaps the most painful aspect of the 'agony of perceivedness' for the Beckettian actor is the lack of a character to mediate the audience's perception of the actor's body and soul. Jonathan Kalb writes that there is a widespread misconception that the difficulty of acting the great classic roles such as

Left: the RSC production of *Endgame* by Donald McWhinnie at the Aldwych Theatre (1964).

Opposite page: the National Theatre production of *Play* by George Devine at the Old Vic (1964).

Hamlet, Lear, and Medea 'has to do with the powers of mimesis'.[79] 'What makes such roles daunting', Kalb explains,

is not the depictive problem of the characters' opaque surfaces – the fictional personas are really not so difficult to embody – but rather the deeper problem of transparency, the quality in them that denudes the actor and reveals the degree of sophistication in his or her experience. The dignity in great performances is always to some extent non-representational, and in this sense all of Beckett's plays are actor's 'vehicles'. His theatre always invokes that same fear of or opportunity for exposure. . . . To use a formulation of [Billie] Whitelaw's, actors inevitably 'grin

through' their roles 'like wallpaper (patterns) through distemper'.[80]

The real challenge of acting the great classic roles is not the demands that these roles make on the actor's skill in mimetic imitation or representation (what Kalb calls 'the depictive problem of the characters' opaque surfaces'), but the far more profound challenge imposed on the actor's ability to undergo – that is, to suffer – the deepest and most profound human experiences on demand and in public. The classic roles are psychically painful to actors because the

367

process of embodying Hamlet, Lear, or Medea forces the actor to explore, expose, and reveal to the audience not merely the pathos of a character, but the painful depths of the actor's own soul and psyche.

Beckett's plays are even more psychically challenging to an actor than the classics because the actors are deprived even of the opaque surfaces of their characters to hide behind. Ben Barnes has observed that 'the problem of production' in Beckett's theatre consists of 'convincing the actor to forfeit the notion of character'.[81] Beckett's figures, in both his theatre and prose, are not representations of characters in any conventional sense, but are *loci* from which Beckett stages the evacuation of the subject and the invocation of the void. The self and its manifestations – language, emotion, the physical body – is conceived of as under erasure.

As the narrator says in *The Unnamable*: 'Where I am there is no one but me who is not.'[82] The human being is defined by an absence: 'What I liked in anthropology', says Molloy, 'was its inexhaustible faculty of negation, its relentless definition of man, as though he were no better than God, in terms of what he is not.'[83] Beckett's texts present the abandonment of a coherent subjects and their replacement with the configurations of uncertain subjectivities orbiting around an empty centre. In Beckett's work there is an unending sequence of attempts at production and cancellation of the self; in *Molloy*, *Malone Dies*, and *The Unnamable*, for example, this relentless process of self-production and self-cancellation culminates in a total 'withdrawal into anonymity'.[84]

This process of production and cancellation of the self makes it impossible for the Beckett actor to fashion a coherent and stable sense of character. Even dialogue, which for centuries was the principle means of theatrically constituting a stable and coherent representation of subjectivity, becomes in Beckett's dramaturgy a method of decentering and destabilizing the construction of character. Dialogue in Beckett's plays does not constitute individuality, since there is no sense of words 'belonging' to one character rather than another – as in *Endgame*, where

Clov's words, 'Finished, it's finished, nearly finished, it must be nearly finished', are then reiterated by Hamm: 'It's finished, we're finished. Nearly finished.'[85]

Deprived of a character to play, Beckett actors must confront the audience in their own unmediated presence; the actor in Beckett's theatre must offer his or her own soul and psyche, transparent and exposed to the audience; unable to hide behind the character's mask, Beckett actors are forced to perform their own suffering. As Joseph Chaikin has reported, Beckett forces the actor to connect with the audience '*as a person*'.[86] Moreover, the actor's presence is itself marked by the absence of the expected representational presentation of character.

This 'minus function',[87] resulting from frustration of the expectation of a coherent and stable character, is felt by the audience, drawing attention to the existential presence of the concrete actor whose energy should, but refuses to, cohere into a representation of a consistent human subject. It is also felt, acutely, by the actor, who must present himself to the audience with the knowledge that his own subjectivity is marked by absence and emptiness. For this reason, the actors in Beckett's theatre 'find themselves facing an emptiness on stage that is unbearable for them *as actors*'.[88]

'There's our catastrophe'[89]

Beckett's texts constantly frustrate attempts to stabilize or determine, once and for all, the images and impressions that the texts generate. Reading a Beckett text or seeing a Beckett play is to engage in a process of hermeneutic implosion, in which meanings and interpretations emerge only to be cancelled, ideas emerge only to be negated, and references emerge only to slip away, be hollowed out and ridiculed. An effect of this process of semantic and ideational breakdown is the opening of a pathway to intensities of experience that exceeds referentiality and cannot be translated into cognitive terms.

Psychotherapist Christopher Bollas has persuasively argued that there is a mode of heightened inter-personal communication or sensibility to the other that emerges when cognitive parameters are suspended, disrupted, or shut down.[90] According to Bollas, 'the unconscious can receive experiences from external reality and . . . can also receive the other's unconscious with preconscious intermediation'.[91] When the cognitive process is immobilized or elided, this non-cognitive perception of the other 'results in more sensitive contact with the other and a greater reliance on feelings'.[92]

Bollas's contention that the suspension of cognition opens up possibilities for more intense and deeper experiences of the other is supported by Maurice Merleau-Ponty's observation that 'the existence of other people is a difficulty and an outrage for objective thought'.[93] The breakdown in cognition generated by Beckett's theatre, together with the existential nakedness of the Beckett actor, combines to create an acute and deeply empathetic awareness of the actor's presence. When the actor is then made to suffer in body and soul, as Beckett's *mise en scène* brutally ensures, the impact of the audience's heightened awareness of the actor's real suffering presence is devastating.

The affinity between Greek tragedy and ritual sacrifice has been noted by Sigmund Freud,[94] Rene Girard,[95] and Pierre Vidal-Naquet and Jean-Pierre Vernant.[96] Girard has observed that Aristotle's *Poetics* 'is something of a manual of sacrificial practices'.[97] In the theatre of representational illusion, the sacrifice is enacted as a mimesis or imitation of suffering; in Beckett's theatre, the reality of the actor's suffering means that the actor is a real rather than a mimetic sacrificial victim. The conditions of a Beckett performance require the actors to offer their suffering bodies and their souls to the spectators in an act of genuine sacrifice.

The idea of a theatre of sacrifice is typically associated with the passionate manifestos of Antonin Artaud[98] and Jerzy Grotowski[99] rather than the reserved Beckett – who has, in fact, explicitly distanced himself from Grotowski: 'Not for me these Grotowskis and Methods.'[100] But passion, rhetoric, manifestos, and even denials aside, it is Beckett who has most successfully created a contemporary theatre of sacrifice. Beckett himself seemed to have been aware of the parallel between his theatre and the nexus between tragedy and sacrifice, and the short play *Catastrophe*[101] can be read as his critique of representation and self-critique of his own theatre in staging the agony of performance.

Written in 1982 for *Une nuit pour Vaclav Havel* at the Festival d'Avignon, and dedicated to the then-imprisoned Czech playwright, *Catastrophe* is set in a theatre during the final rehearsal of a play. The action consists of an impatient and pompous figure called 'Director' orchestrating the image of a silent and nearly inert figure called 'Protagonist'. *Catastrophe*'s Director, seated in an armchair and wearing a fur coat and a fur toque, is putting the 'final touches to the last scene'. His female assistant stands beside him, wearing white coveralls, with a pencil poised ready on her ear, prepared to carry out his instructions. Mid-stage, standing on a 'black block eighteen inches high', is Protagonist:

Black wide-brimmed hat. Black dressing-gown to ankles. Barefoot. Head bowed. Age and physique unimportant.

His skull is the colour of ash, and his hands are 'clawlike', 'crippled' with 'fibrous degeneration'. The directorial adjustments to Protagonist cause him to be stripped to his underclothes, his skin whitened, his hands joined together and held waist high, his head bowed. Protagonist is silent and compliant throughout. He shivers ('Bless his heart', says Director), but says nothing; ('Sure he won't utter?' asks the female assistant; 'Not a squeak', says Director).

Director insists that they 'hide the face'. The pedestal is raised. The head is lowered. The lighting cues are set: blackout of general stage light, fade-out of light on Protagonist's body, light on the head alone, long pause. Director now sits in the audience, contemplates his creation, and pronounces it 'Lovely.' The play concludes:

A (*timidly*): What if he were to . . . were to . . . raise his head . . . an instant . . . show his face . . . just an instant.

D: For God's sake! What next? Raise his head? Where do you think we are? In Patagonia? Raise his head? For God's sake! (*Pause.*) Good. There's our catastrophe. In the bag. Once more and I'm off.

A (*to L*): Once more and he's off.

Fade-up of light on P's body. Pause. Fade-up of general light.

D: Stop! (*Pause.*) Now . . . let 'em have it.

Fade-out of general light. Pause. Fade-out of light on body. Light on head alone. Long pause.

Terrific! He'll have them on their feet. I can hear it from here.

Pause. Distant storm of applause. P raises his head, fixes the audience. The applause falters, dies.

Long pause.

Fade-out of light on face.[102]

Catastrophe can of course be understood as an allegory of political tyranny, a dramatization of the conditions of the artist in a totalitarian state, ending in a final, stirring gesture of silent defiance. But as Anthony Kubiak has noted, in Catastrophe the tyranny of the state and the tyranny of the theatre itself 'bleed almost inperceptively into one another'.[103] Moreover, the play staged by the Director and his assistant in Catastrophe is much more like a play by Beckett himself than that of any official playwright of a totalitarian regime.

Given what we know of Beckett's work as a playwright and director, Catastrophe, despite its dedication and the occasion of its first production, appears to be less a critique of political terror than an ironic and devastating self-critique of the terror of tragic representation. Catastrophe presents the actor as a human sacrifice offered to create an 'overwhelming powerful image' of suffering. Placed on an altar (a 'black block eighteen inches high') and painted, the actor's suffering is aestheticized and given to the audience as the 'visual poetry' of pain. The Director ensures that the audience is able to see as much of the actor as possible, while still preserving the illusion that the actor's suffering is not real. Protagonist's face, like the reality of the actor's sacrifice, must remain hidden: 'Raise his head? For God's sake! (*Pause.*) Good. There's our catastrophe.'

Catastrophe exposes the source of the spectators' intense emotional response to Beckett's theatre: the demands that Beckett's *mise en scène* place on his actors force them to become, like the Nietzschean tragic hero and the Greek *pharmakos*, a sacrifice whose suffering brings an experience of transformation, silence, and awe to those for whom they suffer. Contrary to the assumption of traditional performance that the production of empathy requires the actor's presence to be subsumed into the representation of character, Beckett's theatre engenders powerful empathetic response precisely because of its subversion of representation and negation of character.

What is decisive to the emotional impact of Beckett's theatre is the way in which the *mise en scène* and the process of negation and cancellation is constructed to ensure that the fictional suffering of his stage figure is existentially present as the real physical and spiritual suffering of the actor. The final gesture of Catastrophe's Protagonist recalls both Billie Whitelaw's testimony that Beckett actors 'inevitably 'grin through' their roles 'like wallpaper (patterns) through distemper',[104] and Artaud's invocation of the actor as a sacrificial offering 'burnt at the stake, signalling through the flames'.[105] The silence of the audience at the end of Catastrophe is the silence of awe – the silence of experiencing the transformative power of real human sacrifice.

Notes and References

1. Jean-François Lyotard, *The Postmodern Condition: a Report on Knowledge*, trans. G. Bennington and B. Massumi (Minneapolis: University of Minnesota Press, 1984), p. xxiv.

2. Fredric Jameson, 'Postmodernism, or the Cultural Logic of Late Capitalism', p. 69.

3. Samuel Beckett, 'Play', in *Collected Shorter Plays* (New York: Grove Press, 1984), p. 157.

4. Judith Butler, *Excitable Speech: a Politics of the Performative* (New York: Routledge, 1997), p. 10, quoting Shoshana Felman, *The Literary Speech Act: Don Juan with J. L. Auston, or Seduction in Two Languages*, trans. Catherine Porter (Ithaca: Cornell University Press, 1983), p. 94.

5. Pierre Bourdieu, *The Logic of Practice*, trans. Richard Nice (Stanford: Stanford University Press, 1990), p. 73.

6. 'By "empathy" I mean "a capacity or disposition to know, to feel, and to respond congruently to what

another is feeling, and the process of doing so".' See Carl Plantinga, 'The Scene of Empathy and the Human Face on Film', in *Passionate Views: Film, Cognition, and Emotion*, ed. Carl Plantiga and Greg M. Smith (Baltimore: Johns Hopkins University Press, 1999), p. 245.

7. Martin Esslin, *The Theatre of the Absurd* (New York: Pelican, 1968), p. 300. See also Martin Esslin, 'Godot, the Authorized Version', *Journal of Beckett Studies*, I (Winter 1976), p. 99, where Esslin repeats his view that Beckett achieves 'a genuine *Verfremdungseffekt*'.

8. Ibid.

9. Samuel Beckett, *Endgame* (New York: Grove Press, 1958), p. 2.

10. Ibid., p. 301.

11. Jacques Derrida, *Of Grammatology*, trans. Gaytari Chekravorty Spivak (Baltimore: Johns Hopkins University Press, 1976), p. 65.

12. Denis Diderot, 'Conversations on the Natural Son', in *Selected Writings on Art and Literature*, trans. G. Bremmer (London: Penguin Books, 1994).

13. Peter Szondi, *Theory of the Modern Drama*, trans. Michael Hays (Minneapolis: University of Minnesota Press, 1987), p. 8.

14. Ibid.

15. Vasily Osipovish Torporkov, *Stanislavski in Rehearsal: the Final Years*, trans. C. Edwards (New York: Theatre Arts Books, 1979), p. 101.

16. Ibid., p. 14.

17. Robert Cohen, *Theatre* (Mountain View, California: Mayfield, 1997), p. 24 (Cohen's emphasis).

18. Bruce Wilshire, *Role Playing and Identity: the Limits of Theatre as Metaphor* (Bloomington; Indianapolis: University of Indiana Press, 1982), p. 27–8 (emphasis added).

19. In film, the media through which most people now experience acting, the disappearance of the actor in the persona of the character is taken for granted. As film theorist Christian Metz has observed, the spectator of a realist film engages in a leap 'from an objectively real but denied signifier to an imaginary but psychologically real signified' as the fiction of the signified role cancels the spectator's perception of the signifying actor. See Christian Metz, *The Imaginary Signifier: Psychoanalysis and the Cinema*, trans. Celia Britton, Annwyl Williams, Ben Brewster, and Alfred Guzzetti (Bloomington: Indiana University Press, 1982), p. 116.

20. Bertolt Brecht, 'Notes on Stanislavsky', *Tulane Drama Review*, IX, No. 2 (Winter 1964), p. 155.

21. Bertolt Brecht, *Brecht on Theatre*, ed. John Willett (New York: Hill and Wang, 1964), p. 37–8.

22. Marvin Carlson, *Theories of the Theatre: a Historical and Critical Survey from the Greeks to the Present* (Ithaca; London: Cornell University Press, 1994), p. 385.

23. Douglas Kellner, 'Brecht's Marxist Aesthetic: the Korch Connection', in *Bertolt Brecht: Political Theory and Literary Practice*, ed. Betty Nancy Weber and Hubert Heinin (Athens: University of Georgia Press, 1980), p. 32.

24. Beckett, *The Unnamable*, p. 298.

25. Robert Weimann, 'Representation and Performance: the Uses of Authority in Shakespeare's Theatre', *PMLA*, CI, No. 3 (May 1992), p. 499.

26. Wolfgang Iser, *The Act of Reading* (Baltimore; London: Johns Hopkins University Press, 1978), p. 169.

27. Weimann, 'Representation and Performance', p. 499.

28. Wolfgang Iser, 'The Art of Failure: the Stifled Laugh in Beckett's Theatre', in *Prospecting: from Reader Response to Literary Anthropology* (Baltimore; London: Johns Hopkins University Press, 1993), p. 190.

29. Joseph Chaikin, *The Presence of the Actor: Notes on the Open Theater, Disguises, Acting, and Repression* (New York: Athenaeum, 1972), p. 138.

30. Brecht, *Brecht on Theatre*, p. 138.

31. Martin Esslin, *Meditations: Essays on Brecht, Beckett, and the Media* (New York: Grove Press, 1982), p. 123 (Esslin's emphasis).

32. Samuel Beckett, *Watt* (London: Calder, 1953), p. 75–6 (emphasis added).

33. Jonathan Kalb, *Beckett in Performance* (Cambridge: Cambridge University Press, 1989), p. 235.

34. Ibid., p. 234.

35. Chaikin, *The Presence of the Actor*, p. 138 (emphasis added).

36. James Knowlson, *Damned to Fame: the Life of Samuel Beckett* (London: Bloomsbury, 1996), p. 502.

37. Ibid.

38. Ibid.

39. Kalb, *Beckett in Performance*, p. 198.

40. Ibid.

41. Ibid., p. 199.

42. Ibid., p. 198–9.

43. Ibid., p. 181.

44. Ibid.

45. Ibid., p. 202.

46. Maurice Harmon, ed., *No Author Better Served: the Correspondence of Samuel Beckett and Alan Schneider* (Cambridge: Harvard University Press, 1998), p. 2–5.

47. Ibid.

48. Ibid., p. 11.

49. Beckett, *The Unnamable*, p. 418.

50. H. Porter Abbot, 'Tyranny and Theatricality: the Example of Samuel Beckett', *Theatre Journal*, XL, No. 1 (1988), p. 82.

51. Ibid.

52. Chaikin, *The Presence of the Actor*, p. 145.

53. Beckett, *Endgame*, p. 1.

54. Ibid.

55. Samuel Beckett, *Happy Days* (New York: Grove Press, 1961), p. 7.

56. Beckett, 'Play', in *Collected Shorter Plays*, p. 1.

57. Samuel Beckett, 'Krapp's Last Tape', in *Collected Shorter Plays*, p. 55.

58. Samuel Beckett, 'Quad,' in *Collected Shorter Plays*, p. 291, 293.

59. Knowlson, *Damned to Fame*, p. 516.

60. Kalb, *Beckett in Performance*, p. 203.

61. Beckett, 'Molloy', in *Molloy, Malone Dies, The Unnamable*, p. 157.

62. Gabriele Schwab, *Subjects without Selves: Transitional Texts in Modern Fiction* (Cambridge: Harvard University Press, 1994), p. 140.

63. Samuel Beckett, 'The Lost Ones', in *The Complete Short Prose, 1929–1989*, ed. S. E. Gontarski (New York: Grove Press, 1995), p. 219.

64. Kalb, *Beckett in Performance*, p. 147.

65. Ibid., p. 234.

66. Ibid., p. 235.

67. Eileen Blumenthal, *Joseph Chaikin: Exploring at the Boundaries of Theatre* (Cambridge: Cambridge University Press, 1984), p. 188.

68. Kalb, *Beckett in Performance*, p. 59.

69. Samuel Beckett, 'Film', in *Collected Shorter Plays*, p. 163, 165.

70. Beckett, 'Play', in *Collected Shorter Plays*, p. 147.

71. Ibid., p. 157.

72. Ibid.

73. Beckett, *Happy Days*, p. 7.

74. Beckett, '*Molloy*', in *Molloy, Malone Dies, The Unnamable*, p. 88.

75. Beckett, '*Play*', in *Collected Shorter Plays*, p. 154.

76. Ibid., p. 157.

77. Beckett, *Happy Days*, p. 20–1, 25–9.

78. Beckett, *Waiting for Godot*, p. 49.

79. Kalb, *Beckett in Performance*, p. 146.

80. Ibid.

81. Ben Barnes, 'Aspects of Directing Beckett', *Irish University Review*, XIV, No. 1 (1984), p. 86.

82. Samuel Beckett, *The Unnamable* (New York: Grove Press, 1958), p. 94.

83. Beckett, '*Molloy*', in *Molloy, Malone Dies, The Unnamable*, p. 39.

84. Wolfgang Iser, *The Implied Reader: Patterns of Communication in Prose Fiction from Bunyan to Beckett* (Baltimore; London: Johns Hopkins University Press, 1974), p. 164, 264.

85. Beckett, *Endgame*, p. 1, 50.

86. Chaikin, *The Presence of the Actor*, p. 138 (emphasis added).

87. Iser, 'The Art of Failure', p. 158.

88. Kalb, *Beckett in Performance*, p. 146.

89. Samuel Beckett, '*Catastrophe*', in *Collected Shorter Plays*, p. 300.

90. Christopher Bollas, *Cracking Up: the Work of Unconscious Experience* (London: Routledge, 1995), p. 10–11, 14-16. See also Christopher Bollas, *The Shadow of the Object: Psychoanalysis and the Unthought Known* (New York: Columbia University Press, 1987), p. 16–17; *Forces of Destiny: Psychoanalysis and the Human Idiom* (London: Free Association Books, 1989), p. 213–14.

91. Bollas, *Cracking Up*, p. 11.

92. Ibid., p. 15.

93. Maurice Merleau-Ponty, *Phenomenology of Perception*, trans. Colin Smith (London: Routledge, 1989), p. 349.

94. Sigmund Freud, *Totem and Taboo: Some Points of Agreement Between the Mental Lives of Savages and Neurotics*, trans. James Strachey (New York: Norton, 1950), p. 192–4.

95. Rene Girard, *Violence and the Sacred*, trans. Patrick Gregory (Stanford: Stanford University Press, 1977), p. 68–88, 290–7.

96. Jean-Pierre Vernant and Pierre Vidal-Naquet, *Myth and Tragedy in Ancient Greece*, trans. Janet Lloyd (New York: Zone Books, 1990).

97. Girard, *Violence and the Sacred*, p. 291.

98. Antonin Artaud, *The Theatre and Its Double*, trans. Mary Caroline Richards (New York: Grove Press, 1958).

99. Jerzy Grotowski, *Towards a Poor Theatre* (New York: Simon and Schuster, 1968).

100. Kalb, *Beckett in Performance*, p. 249.

101. Beckett, '*Catastrophe*', in *Collected Shorter Plays*, p. 295–301.

102. Ibid., p. 300–1.

103. Anthony Kubiak, *Stages of Terror: Terrorism, Ideology, and Coercion as Theatre History* (Bloomington; Indianapolis: Indiana University Press, 1991), p. 134.

104. Kalb, *Beckett in Performance*, p. 146.

105. Artaud, *The Theatre and Its Double*, p. 13.

Adrienne Scullion

Self and Nation: Issues of Identity in Modern Scottish Drama by Women

The creation of the devolved Scottish parliament in 1999, argues Adrienne Scullion, has the potential to change everything that has been understood and imagined or thought and speculated about Scotland. The devolved parliament shifts the governance of the country, resets financial provisions and socio-economic management, recreates Scottish politics and Scottish society – and affects how Scotland is represented and imagined by artists of all kinds. The radical context of devolution should also afford Scottish criticism an unprecedented opportunity to rethink its more rigid paradigms and structures. Specifically, this article questions what impact political devolution might have on the rhetoric of Scottish cultural criticism by paralleling feminist analysis of three plays by women premiered in Scotland in 2000 with the flexible, even hybrid, model of the nation afford by devolution, resetting identity within Scottish culture as much less predictable and much more inclusive than has previously been understood. An earlier version was delivered by the author on 5 March 2001 to the Royal Society of Edinburgh in receipt of the biennial RSE/BP Prize Lectureship in the Humanities. Adrienne Scullion teaches in the Department of Theatre, Film and Television Studies at the University of Glasgow, where she is also the academic director of the Centre for Cultural Policy Research.

ANGEL [*a Bulgarian ship's engineer*]: Remember when the Rooskies had their coup? When Yeltsin stopped the tanks? For 'democracy'! Well, the next day we went over to the Suloy. Remember her?

NATKA [*a Bulgarian fish gutter*]: Rooskie bucket!

ANGEL: She was anchored off Bressay. The Suloy crew had promised us new videos, we were sick of our old videos. So we take the dinghy. Wind, rain, bloody hell, waves up, down, up, down. But when we get to the Suloy there's someone high up on the funnel; he's unscrewing the hammer and sickle from the funnel. I say to the Rooskies tell that guy watch out – wait till our dinghy's clear. If that lump of metal hit us – boom – we go with it to the bottom of the sea. And one of the Rooskies, he says: You think we're crazy? You think we throw this in the sea? So today Moscow radios: 'Take down hammer and sickle, destroy immediately.' But what do we know? Maybe Friday, maybe next month, maybe three months' time – Moscow radios again: 'Put back hammer and sickle. Immediately.' And where would we be?

(Sue Glover, *Shetland Saga* I, iii, p. 24–5)[1]

THE CREATION and implementation of the devolved Scottish parliament marks a radical reorganization and recreation of British political structures. It alters our whole understanding of and relationship to government; it brings decision-making closer; and it encourages a more immediate sense of responsibility and empowerment on the part of the electorate, on the part of Scottish society.

As a further consequence of these legislative and constitutional changes, the 'imagined' nature of Scotland also shifts: Scottish culture, and within that issues of representation and identity, has been preoccupied with ideas of colonialism, marginalism, and parochialism. But, in a context where a significant degree of political independence has been achieved, the dynamic must shift from aspiration and desire to definition and responsibility. The fact of the Holyrood government will result in shifts in how we understand and participate in the dynamic processes of Scottish national identity.

This essay considers representation and identity in recent Scottish drama against the backdrop of political and legislative devolution. It is in two parts: the first part is a brief overview of the ideas and engagements with national identity within modern critical literature – and, in particular, within Scottish critical literature; and the second considers issues of identity and representation in the drama that emerges from that system.

Three main points underpin this work: that devolution matters in terms of image, representation, and identity, that devolution will shift how we create and imagine and represent Scotland; that identity is a weighty and significant area of concern for artists; and that the work of women artists, for my purposes the work of women dramatists, when writing as if gender matters and with a feminist perspective, can demonstrate new or alternative approaches to conventional representations and conventional narratives. My argument is that in challenging the conventions of narrative or in challenging the conventions of gender, women artists, here women playwrights, also challenge the conventions of representing and responding to the nation.

Ideas of National Identity in Scotland

The dynamics of identity and representation, and in particular national identity and the representation of nation, are key themes across the whole of Scottish culture. In his influential description of the nation as 'an imagined political community', Benedict Anderson outlines a version of belonging which is eclectic, multifarious, and resists closure.[2] He allows for a version of the nation, an identity which is open, egalitarian, and peace loving – this very much in line with the sets of identity that Scottishness would like to claim for itself.

In opposition and in practice, however, the application of the idea of the nation, the actual functioning of states, may be less tolerant; for nations also define themselves as exclusive and sovereign; nations build literal and metaphoric barriers that limit access and regulate membership; nations separate the elect from the ostracized. The point in the establishment of society at which one group, one identity, is legitimized and another is disenfranchised and margin-

alized – cast, however crudely, as 'other' – is a result of the socio-cultural development of the community, a conjunction of historical, economic, social, and political factors. It is an exclusion defined and described in the nation's traditions, myths, and collective imagination, to be replayed in the nation's cultural texts.

Like any peripheral culture, Scotland expends inordinate amounts of energy defending and defining a sense of national identity to bolster the pervasive economic attraction of the various cultural cores. Politically and economically, Scotland has seemed tied to a series of ideologies and discourses which artists have increasingly found to be restrictive in depicting their own experiences and their own fantasies, *and* which critics too have found reductive and limiting.

The dominant, or at least the significantly pervasive, representations of 'tartanry', 'kailyard', and 'Clydeside', for example, provide highly marketable, if conventional and even regressive, representations of Scots and Scotland. They elicit a predictable series of representations and narratives, with each being played out against their preferred topographies of cityscape and rural landscape.

But images, representations, and identities do not emerge unbidden or from thin air. As critics like Craig Beveridge and Ronald Turnbull, Cairns Craig, and David McCrone have argued, these familiar representations are based on the economic, social, and historical realities of Scotland.[3] However, within an expanding arts and broadcasting industry, within an artistically varied and diverse Scottish culture, writers and directors are increasingly empowered to revisit, reset, and re-use these traditions and emblems. In modern Scottish culture the motifs of kailyard and tartanry, of the country and the city, of myth and history, of Enlightenment, war, and democracy are being investigated in new ways.

For example, the potential for re-reading and re-presenting the preferred identities of Scottish culture allows unexpected engagements with satire, irony, and critical and reflexive deconstruction – as in the raucous satire of *Rab C. Nesbitt* (BBC, 1989–99), the somewhat surreal irony of *Chewin' the Fat* (BBC, from 1999), or in Iain Heggie's contemporary resetting of Gogol's *Diary of a Madman* as *King of Scotland* (Babel, 2000).

But this resetting has to make more of a difference. If Scottish culture has been seen to be obsessively attracted to a set of easily transferable character stereotypes, ubiquitous images, and predictable politics, then Scottish criticism, it is argued, has merely added to the myopia. And it has done so by validating and perpetuating these debilitating and constraining versions of national and gender identities.[4] It seems axiomatic that if representations and images and identities are evolving within modern Scottish culture, then so too must our critical language, our critical rhetoric and discourse.

In recent years the critical literature around the idea of identity – and in particular national identity – has shifted. It is commonly argued that the re-emergence of political and ethnic nationalism in Europe and beyond has led historians, social scientists, artists, and critics alike to reconsider issues of identity. This has led to an interrogation of the critical orthodoxies of cultural imperialism, colonialism, marginalization, and their neat binary oppositions. The ideas of nations as 'imagined communities' and of identity in modern societies – in modern Britain – as fragmentary and 'fuzzy' have significant ubiquity when considering the evolution of identity politics and its impact on our critical vocabulary.[5]

The huge changes in the political life of Scotland build on history and on the traditions and institutions of the existing and independent civil society; but these changes also create new structures, new modes of organization, and new policies. Similarly, national identity in Scotland has achieved an odd balance of, on the one hand, the historically and politically fixed and certain, and, on the other, the new, the quixotic, and the opportunistic. This presents a brand-new context, a brand-new symbiosis of producer and product, and of infrastructure or institution and representation.

If we agree that it is important to monitor and challenge the policy, the legislative and institutional effects of devolution, then it is equally important to interrogate the images, representations, and identities that emerge from this new context.

Gender and Issues of the 'National'

In relation to gender: David McCrone is one of the many commentators who identify and describe the phallocentricity of Scottish culture. He suggests that this has limited or at least constrained the palette of identities available to Scottish artists and that, as a result, there has been an inevitable tendency to regulate the roles available to characters, to reduce the stories they can tell. In this, he argues, the depiction of women has been particularly vulnerable – being relegated 'to walk-on parts', to roles as 'keepers of the moral and family values of the nation'[6] – for example, Chris Guthrie in *Sunset Song* (1932), Peggy in *The Gorbals Story* (Glasgow Unity, 1946), or even Janet in *Dr Finlay's Casebook*.

Certainly the idea of the woman character as the personification of natural, physical, topographic Scotland and, by extension, women as a symptom of and/or metaphor for colonial exploitation has been a particularly favoured symbol within Scottish representations: for example, Flora MacIvor in Walter Scott's *Waverley* (1814), the woman in Jessie Kesson's *Another Time, Another Place* (1983), or more recently Mary Macgregor in the film version of *Rob Roy* directed by Michael Caton Jones (1995)).[7]

But such assumptions and readings are predicated upon patriarchal and indeed on colonial models of experience and criticism. And they do not go unrecognized or unopposed. At the very least, the assumptions of patriarchy are challenged by feminist artists and by feminist criticism. But what about the impact of new politics, what about the impact of devolution? Doesn't that demand an equally subversive criticism? Can the new politics produce a parallel questioning of political orthodoxy and of the construction of the nation? What is there is in contemporary Scottish criticism that truly engages with the nature of devolution and begins to facilitate a new critical paradigm for a post-devolution culture?

And a further example in relation to the nation: it has also been argued that cultural theory in Scotland, perhaps even cultural policy, reaches an impasse because it still desires to find a Scottish 'national culture', when, in the context of new nationalisms, new federalisms, 'fuzzy frontiers' and globalization, this is an 'illegitimate' project.

A more useful agenda, it is suggested, is one willing to acknowledge that modern societies do not experience 'a national culture', but are essentially 'pluralistic' and paradoxical.[8] A more useful agenda is one willing to acknowledge that society cannot achieve 'an integrated discourse which will connect with political and social realities' but can – perhaps even *should* – aspire to a cultural project that is flexible, inclusive, democratic.[9] And the question here would be: could a post-devolution critical rhetoric support this model?[10]

Representation and Identity

Within the context of devolution, the Scottish Executive has the responsibility to monitor and underwrite the organization and the funding of many of the cultural industries of Scotland. But, in addition, the Holyrood parliament challenges artists. In an article written for *The Scotsman* in 1997, in the aftermath of the devolution referendum, two of Scotland's leading playwrights, David Greig and David Harrower, commented on the creative potential of a new political environment:

Scotland has voted to redefine itself as a nation. To redefine ourselves we need to understand ourselves, exchange ideas and aspirations, confront enduring myths, expose injustices, and explore our past. The quality, accessibility, and immediacy of Scottish theatre make it one of the best arenas in which these dialogues can take place.[11]

Greig and Harrower's acknowledgement of the social and cultural responsibilities of the artist, and in particular of the playwright, underlines the fact that much of contemporary Scottish theatre has the ambition to be a site of both political and social debate,

and aesthetic and dramaturgical innovation and experiment. It is certainly the case that the writers and the directors of new theatre in Scotland have set themselves an agenda very different from the fashion-victim, violent-chic introspection of contemporary London theatre, perhaps from a fuller awareness of the significance of representation within a culture in political flux and of limited financial resources. In a wider context of change and adaptation, contemporary Scottish dramatists are increasingly able to experiment with historical and geographical settings and with character and narrative conventions, as well as to challenge the orthodoxies of what it might mean to write a 'Scottish play', what it might mean to make theatre in and of Scotland.

Writing some six years ago, one of the key issues that I then dealt with as a critic of twentieth-century Scottish drama was the nature – or at least the narrative – of community, and the parameters of gender and national identity. Then, I described that concern in terms of the nature and the politics of belonging. I noted that this was a common feature in modern Scottish drama, where the moment of inclusion or exclusion from the community seemed to be a recurrent narrative motif, where the lines of the elect or the ostracized seemed both predictable and rigid.[12] These themes, these moments, are still significant in more recent drama. But I am now interested in re-framing that same concern by taking on board the potentiality of devolution to shift representation, identity, and criticism, and to redefine the community as more flexible and as less rigid.

I want to begin this critical project with reference to three plays from the year 2000: Zinnie Harris's *Further than the Furthest Thing*, which premiered on 6 August at the Traverse Theatre in Edinburgh in a co-production by the Tron Theatre and the Royal National Theatre directed by Irina Brown; Sue Glover's *Shetland Saga*, which was premiered on 28 July by and at the Traverse, in a production directed by Philip Howard; and Nicola McCartney's *Home*, which opened on 10 February at the Tron Theatre in Glasgow, in a production directed by Carol Moore for the playwright's own small-scale touring company, Lookout.[13]

'Further than the Furthest Thing'

Zinnie Harris's *Further than the Furthest Thing* adopts a very conventional two-act structure, but the setting, as also the characters and their stories, are far from familiar or predictable. The play begins on a remote island somewhere in the middle of the South Atlantic, and the first act concludes with a volcanic eruption, a catastrophic event which forces the total evacuation of the island's population to Southampton – the setting for the second act. The island is a version of Tristan da Cuhna, and the volcanic eruption is based on the one that actually occurred on that island in October 1961. But Harris's main purpose is not to tell that story but to create a space, a distinctive diegetic space, that is physically remote and isolated.

The play describes the impact of violent geological and environmental forces on this edge-of-the-world place and on the lives of four of its inhabitants – the middle-aged couple Mill and Bill, their nephew Francis, and his former lover Rebecca. The play also dramatizes the impact on these characters of other extraordinary external factors – the forces of capital and of empire, and of violent masculinity – also working through ideas of belonging and the nature and the function of community, the nature and function of identity.

From the start of the play the islanders are a community set apart, most obviously geographically. As a group and as individuals they have experienced only limited interventions from the outside world. Theirs is a society that has evolved gradually and opportunistically over the centuries. As a result their identity is a hybrid one, with an ecology framed and sustained by the island itself. External markers such as dress, diet, customs, and language demonstrate the islanders' distinctiveness, as do their shared beliefs, myths, memories, and history. In addition to an immediate and even localized identity as islanders, the community also has an identity as a colony, as part of imperial Britain.

The linguistic and semiotic markers of the island claim an authenticity of geography and ecology. The signifiers of their identity are rooted within a clearly delineated geographical space and a lifestyle organized around nature and the agricultural calendar, around more or less predictable climatic changes, but challenged by utterly unpredictable geological forces. Island identity is linked to a cautious equilibrium with the natural world that is violently disrupted by a raft of thematically interconnected external forces – most obviously by the eruption of the volcano, but also by the ambitions of individual entrepreneurs and international business to commercialize the island's natural resources, by the opportunism of governments that want to keep the population away from the island so that it can be used as a military testing ground, and by the sexual assault on one island woman by a group of visiting sailors.

In performance, perhaps the most distinctive marker of island identity is the language Harris gives her characters. This is a highly artificial form of speech that mixes archaic and baroque English with earnest and direct plain speaking: it is full of eccentric pronunciations, emphases, and aspirates, with a grammar of unexpected negatives, plurals, and singulars, in which odd subject and object agreements and disagreements proliferate. This is established in the opening exchange between Mill, the strong, sexy middle-aged woman at the centre of the play, and her nephew Francis:

MILL: Been waiting. Since sun is first come up.
    I's seeing your ship from the first it was.
    I's holding my breath for the rocks.
    Shutting my eyes for the corner.
    Counting my heart's beating as in it came.

FRANCIS: Mill . . .

MILL: Don't come near, just as yet.
    Let me be seeing you first
    The other way
    So these is what they is wearing,
    H'outside there then? . . .

FRANCIS: Only been gone . . .

MILL: Months
   Months and months
   I is counted Francis
   Is half the year and half again.

   (*Further than the Furthest Thing*, I, ii, p. 5–6)[14]

Harris creates a distinctive performative space for her narrative through this heightened aural diegesis. But language here aims at more than overt theatricality. Language also distils and symbolizes the play's narrative: it acts as a metaphor for the narrative crises of the plot, delineating community and marking belonging. Language allows Harris's characters to perform their distinctiveness as individuals *and* as community. It allows characters to communicate individualized and subjective meanings, their own ideas, their own feelings. But simultaneously it also functions in an overt and externalized manner, demonstrating a collective and shared identity.

The islanders use language very precisely and as a medium of fact, of truth: something said is something true, once spoken; uncertainty is cut away. This very precise, metonymic use of language – implicitly linked to a moral code or a system of beliefs – marks the islanders as a very different type of community from that of the outsiders in the play. It also marks this community as significantly and perhaps morally incomprehensible to outsiders. It is an organic language that embodies identity, and that shows the community as distinctive but not, at this stage, as other.

The function of language outside, the use made of language by the outsiders, is quite different. Beyond the island, words have a connotative element, and can mean or even more problematically *suggest* something other than what they signify. Outside language has the potential to be imprecise, to be uncertain, to be duplicitous. In fact the outsiders collude to exploit and deceive the islanders through their different use of and relationship to language: the sailors who raped Rebecca, and refused to listen to her pleas for them to stop, are paralleled with the outside authorities who similarly refuse to listen to the islanders' request to return

to the island; indeed, not only do these outsiders refuse to listen to the islanders, they go so far as to lie about the extent of the damage done by the volcanic eruption.

In addition to these clear refusals to listen and the overt lies, the subtextual nature of outside language acts as a significant point of contrast and miscommunication: and this is underlined by the figure of Mr. Hansen, the one non-islander we meet in the play – an alien figure, with his clear and perfect English, who disrupts and unsettles linguistic identity just as much as the eruption of the volcano disrupts their topographical identity.

During his first encounter with Mill and Bill, Mr. Hansen performs a magic trick that seems to turn an eggshell into a glass jar, then into a completely different egg, and then into a handful of coins. Mill is left completely bemused by the transformation and the seeming disappearance of the eggshell. But it is just sleight of hand, the trick of a skilful conjuror. At the end of his magic routine there seems to be no eggshell and no jar, and Mr. Hansen pockets the coins. The sequence of 'transformations' acts as a neat metaphor for his plans to exploit the natural resources of the island: taking the crayfish (represented by the 'pinnawin' eggshell); bottling it for export (the jar); and taking the profit (the coins).

But, this metaphor of capital aside, Mill's confusion is neither ignorance nor innocence, but a direct result of a way of seeing which is literal and material: in her worldview things do not just disappear; things are what they are, and by extension words mean what they say. In contrast. actions and language outside the island are slippery and even dangerous. Outside the island language has the potential to be imprecise, to be uncertain, to be duplicitous. Words can turn on their user to entrap and condemn.

Language and Otherness

The play dramatizes a community and an identity under pressure, and this is enacted in the shifts in the islanders' use of and relationship to language. In the first act the language marks the solidarity and strength of the community. In the second act, in Southampton, the islanders' identity – so closely tied to the physical reality of the island – begins to fragment and shift: in their new environment their life-style, their language, even their bearing and their appearance, are all changed. This is represented in terms of language that becomes pressurized and even fractures. In Southampton Francis's language becomes more anglicized, more ordered, more structured. He can interpret the potential duplicity of language; and it is this, along with his ability to separate himself as subject of his speech, that marks and increases his separation from the other islanders.

Rebecca is pursued by reporters looking for a story, seeking to elicit words that might go to prove the complete otherness of the islanders. She understands that words can be turned and used against her, but she has neither the linguistic skills nor the psychological propensity to use this to her advantage, and so her only response is the physical one of hitting the reporter.

Bill falls quiet: separated from the island and from the topographical and physical reality of the community, his language becomes inappropriate, invalid. For Southampton, it does not work: it cannot describe what it is he sees and how it is he feels. He is silenced. In contrast, but derived from the same linguistic crisis, Mill's experience in the city leads to an extraordinary explosion of speech: her identity, her language, has also been constrained by the experience of Southampton, but her response is to reassert the voice of the island.

Identity is shaped by history, by collective memory, by shared recollections and traditions. Mill's explosive speech in Act Two recounts one of the community's most awful events. The island had been forgotten during the war, and no supplies had been sent. Months, even years, passed and food stocks dwindled. In order for the majority to survive, the community drew lots and selected seventeen of their number who were then abandoned to starve on a remote part of the island. Mill's retelling of this defining moment of community is the emotional climax of the play. And it is, of course, not just that she speaks, but that she speaks in her own language, and that she retells one of the privileged moments of the community.

Mill's speech finally exposes the 'otherness' of the islanders, at least in the context of Southampton and of modern England. This otherness is achieved through and demonstrated in a combination of the form and the style and the sound of the language, and its ubiquity in telling the myths and history of its own community.

The Return of the Native

One of the key narrative and thematic concerns of this play – one of the key mythologies of community, indeed of nationhood – is the idea and the enactment of the return of the native. This is an element, a theme, and sometimes a character recognizable across the whole of Scottish culture (which frequently tells of the return from the sea, the return of the soldier or the economic emigrant) and across a range of Scottish drama. The theme is discernible in plays as diverse as Stephen Greenhorn's *The Salt Wound* (7:84, 1994), David Harrower's *Kill the Old Torture their Young* (Traverse, 1998), or Stuart Paterson's *King of the Fields* (Traverse, 1999), and it appears as a less overt but still important motif in Aileen Ritchie's *The Juju Girl* (Traverse, 1999) and Peter Arnott's *A Little Rain* (7:84, 2000).

Further than the Furthest Thing dramatizes and remembers several returns. Indeed, in Harris's version the role and the idea structure the entire play – which loops from the return of Francis to the island at the start of the play, to the evacuation of the islanders because of the volcano at the end of Act One, and finally to the return of the evacuees at the end of the second, concluding act.

Firstly and most obviously, then, comes the return of Francis, the ambitious and potent young man. This is a classic, even conventional return of the native – a trope recurrent within all marginalized and peripheral cultures. Francis is here the explorer, the economic emigrant whose return is celebrated and valorized, mythologized and demonized. Conventionally the returning native carries with him values and influences from the external world that unsettle and disrupt the 'old country'. In this narrative of 'the return of the native' one often see the parallelling of 'here' and 'there', of 'old' and 'modern', 'barbaric' and 'civilized', 'trustworthy' and 'untrustworthy', and other positive and negative comparisons.

Certainly, these binary oppositions play an important part in *Further than the Furthest Thing*, which contrasts the island with the outside through structure, narrative, character, and theme. The returning Francis carries a whole raft of these oppositions, casting the island as old-fashioned, backward-looking, uncivilized. But in this play Francis does more than represent the ideas and values of the other place: he is shadowed, even haunted, by a personification of this outside world, as he brings with him the rather mysterious and quite literally other-worldly Mr. Hansen. It is not within the scope of this analysis to comment at length on this figure, but it is certainly the case that his role is far from conventional, and that he too comes into crisis as he renegotiates an identity in some sense caught between the communities of the islanders and that of Southampton.

But there are other returns in this play. The remembered return of Bill grows in significance through the play. Bill left the island after the long hiatus of supply ships and the deaths of the seventeen islanders. He leaves to see the war that has cost the island so much, and when he returns to the island it is with Christianity: he builds a church and everyone on the island is baptized in a effort to cleanse the island from the sin of the deaths. Like Francis he returns with a set of values that constructs the island negatively – as pagan, as barbaric. His solution is to impose a more or less benign version of Christianity. But one might question just how different, at least in structural terms, this means of civilization is to the creed of capitalism and commercial exploitation of the natural resources of the island that Francis promotes on his return.

The second act is dominated by the desire to return to the island. Mill's retelling of

secrets and the death of Bill finally bring it about. His death, as the community's self-appointed chaplain, has a sacrificial element, particularly since he dies in the scalding water of Mr. Hansen's factory pumps. Just as the group of seventeen were sacrificed for the whole society to survive, so in their different ways Bill and, indeed, Francis – who chooses to remain in England – are sacrificed so that the larger group can return to their multi-layered and complex identities on the island, rather than sustain the reduced role of alien and savage that Englishness prefers for them.

The Island and the Crisis of Colonialism

A further and over-arching return maps back to ideas of colonialism. The island is a peripheral and remote outpost of western civilization, and in this the evacuation to Southampton may be understood as a return to the imperial core – which in this case is, of course, England. While the islanders' language is based on a version of English, so too are other visual markers of their identity – including the magazine pictures of the Queen that decorate Mill's island home.

In a model that privileges this colonial paradigm and the idea of the return to the birthplace of empire, the second act of the play confronts the impossibility of the colonized being integrated as equal partners into the social and cultural experience of the economic centre. The colonial power demands that its subjects divest themselves of all identities other than that of the core, as when Mr. Hansen tells Mill:

> It is to do with attitude, Mr Cavendish and
>   his team
> They want you to know you are Britons
> You know what I am talking about
> Start dressing a bit like Britons
> Even when you are by yourself feel like Britons
> At night
> Even when you are undressed, that is the thing.
> When you are naked
> Be Britons even under all the layers
> (II, vi, p. 133)

But this is an identity that the islanders cannot convincingly adopt. Their island identity has not been stripped away, leaving a clean slate for new markers, new identities. Instead it lies subdued and buried beneath the weight of oppressive Englishness, beneath the weight of colonial expectation. Although the islanders do try to use the external signifiers of their new society – changing their dress and their diet, even changing their physicality, their deportment – there are still gaps. In contrast to the organic identities of the island, the imposed markers of England and of Englishness are aggressive and over-determined:

MILL: Be pouring Francis some H'england tea out of the H'england pot Rebecca. Gently.

FRANCIS: I haven't got long.

MILL: Spend a minute Francis.

Rebecca pours some H'england tea.

MILL: And using the H'england saucers Rebecca and giving Francis some H'england milk out of the H'england jug. . . .

Rebecca be giving Francis a H'england biscuit out of the H'england jar. . . .

Rebecca be giving Francis some more H'england tea,
And a bit of H'england sugar.

(II, vii, p. 137–9)

The islanders' attempts to use the totems, the signs and the codes of Englishness remain externalized – the tea things, the deckchairs in Mill and Bill's garden, even the performance of politeness and manners, are distanciated, separate manifestations of a culture that is oppressive and subjugating. But while the islanders at least attempt to use the props of England, they refuse the ambiguity of its language. In applying the precision of her island language to her English environment Mill here disrupts and unsettles not just the English language but Englishness itself.

Harris, then, writes a play this is about crisis in identity, but the *crisis* is not that of the islanders but of England – the crisis in identity is not of the periphery, but of the colonizer who insists on definitions of belonging that are based on absolutes and categorizations. In contrast the hybrid, eclectic identities of the island are significantly inclusive of difference.

My attempt here is not to map onto the play another binary opposition, of colonizer and colonized – and I certainly don't want to suggest that in this there is an easy metaphor for Scotland and Englishness. But I do want to see in the play something of the debate about communities that I said was a significant and recurring feature in Scottish culture. The play contrasts different communities, different ways of belonging, different ways of constructing and demonstrating identity. But the belonging is not essential, it is not absolute. If the islanders are excluded from empire and nation, then, Harris argues, there are other cores of belonging.

What seems significant in *Further than the Furthest Thing* – and indeed in *Shetland Saga* and in *Home* – is that these alternative belongings, these alternative communities, are smaller, more knowable, rather more domestic, perhaps more securely feminine, than previous models of belonging allowed. In passing, and perhaps strengthening this point, it is, of course, the women, Mill and Rebecca, who more successfully mediate the culture of England and who return to the island – without their men, but with a purpose to recreate their community. This potential feminization of the community is a significant evolution wherein the feminine community has traditionally been perceived as separate and other.[15]

'Shetland Saga'

Sue Glover's *Shetland Saga* presents a more naturalistic and even literal approach to ideas of identity. *Shetland Saga* tells of a group of Bulgarian sailors whose fishing ship is anchored indefinitely in Shetland and of their relations with the local community. The play is also very clearly *about* different nationalities, confronting as it does problems of communication, politics, and economics. But *Shetland Saga* is more obviously, more immediately *about* Scottish identity. It is set in Shetland, it has characters who are Scottish, who have a life in Scotland.

But, of course, the Scottishness that Sue Glover describes is just as hybrid as that of the islanders in *Further than the Furthest*

Glover's characters find that these cultural clashes are more containable. As Hoover, the local hotel owner and small businessman, comments early in the play:

> I had a great time in Ullapool. Bloody wonderful! Some Polish celebration or other. Or it might have been a Scottish one. Can't remember.

(I, iii, p. 19)

Now whilst this is clearly a joke, it also raises some of the problems of recognizing and criticizing identity. It is commonly argued that it is in religious or secular ceremonies, in moments of collective celebration through community events, that the markers of identity are most strongly evident. But here Glover recognizes that in post-war, post-industrial, regional Europe the markers of nationhood are at the very least blurred or 'fuzzy' – even in the most heightened and externalized demonstration of community.

The Bulgarians in *Shetland Saga* are trapped in a limbo of political expediency, ideological stand-off, and economic collapse. The ship has only a skeleton crew of three: the two older characters Angel and Natka, experienced sailors, hardened by and adaptable to the unpredictable forces of international politics; and the younger, less experienced Svetan. The three survive on the edge of Europe, on the margins on Shetland society, and on the fringes of the black economy. Their dwindling funds are supplemented by assistance from the local community, but they also scavenge the detritus of western Europe, repairing old electrical goods, salvaging half-empty tins of paint, and doing odd jobs around the town.

Glover shows them gradually being integrated into the social and the economic life of the community as friendships and sexual relations develop – and this is marked through language. Her strategy for distinguishing the speech of the Bulgarians and the speech of the Scots is to have all the characters speak in English but act incomprehension. This convention also allow her to have scenes in which we see miscommunication while hearing the private thoughts of the characters:

From Sue Glover's *Shetland Saga*. Above: Eric Barlow. Opposite page: Anne Lacey and Cas Stewart. Photos: Kevin Low.

Thing: even on the most obvious of levels, the 'Scots' that we meet in Glover's play are firstly 'Shetlanders'. The Scottish identities in *Shetland Saga*, like the identities in *Further than the Furthest Thing*, are elaborate and hybrid, and continue to evolve through connection to other characters, other communities. Glover recognizes that cultural hybridity can lead to an odd blurring of the external markers of national identity. In contrast to Mill's laboured tea ceremony,

MENA: You don't speak any English?

He shakes his head.

Russian?

SVETAN: I'm damned if I'll speak Russian.

MENA: I don't know why I asked you that! It's not as if I speak any –

SVETAN: What's she doing learning Russian?!

MENA: – don't speak anything at all – except Russian –

SVETAN: She learns Russian! From sailors?!

MENA: I'm not English, mind – I'm a Shetlander!

[. . .]

SVETAN: Svetan. Svetan Kralev.

MENA: I don't understand.

SVETAN: Svetan. Svetan Kralev.

MENA: I don't understand.

SVETAN: Svetan.

MENA: Mena. Philomena Jameson.

SVETAN: She meets sailors all the time.

MENA: A girl in every port, I'll bet.

SVETAN: Hundreds of the all the time

[. . .]

SVETAN: I wish – I wish we were somewhere else right now, the two of us. Some place. One language.

MENA: I can feel myself blushing, which is stupid, so stupid. Mena, you're making a fool of yourself.

(I, ii, p. 14–15)

The sailors assert their national identity as Bulgarians, and although this does manifest itself in terms of music, diet, dress, and codes of hospitality, it also tends to be framed in opposition to another identity: that is, they are 'not Russian'. And, of course, 'Russian' here really marks something other than an ethnic identity. But however stridently they claim identity as Bulgarian, they recognize that this is economically and culturally vulnerable: they tend to describe their identity in terms of a place, a country that was home, but one to which they cannot return. Their only connection to this home is via telephone calls, and these are mediated and controlled by the totemic 'phonecards' that quite literally 'count down' relationships.

The sailors are caught by the forces of international capital and by the last gasps of political ideologies conceived of as transnational but now collapsing and being remapped in terms of the twin dynamics of globalization and new nationalism. In contrast to the oppressive weight of the new place, the oppressive weight of Englishness in *Further than the Furthest Thing*, in *Shetland Saga* the new place, the new community, the new identity, and the new language become potentially empowering.

Initially Glover uses language to highlight difference. But the longer the sailors remain in Shetland, the more integrated they become in the local community. And this is signalled in the characters' greater ability to communicate verbally, psychologically, and emotionally. It is not just that the Bulgarians get better at speaking English: all the characters get better at talking honestly and truly. And this is because language works in other ways in this play: and again this is closely connected with what one can say in any given language, in any given community.

For the Bulgarians, language has an extraordinary materiality. If they are to live in Lerwick they must learn its language – they must understand not only the speech of the community and its other signs – its visual codes, its habits and social conventions. But they must also confront the political function of language. Angel, Natka, and Svetan come to recognize the limitations placed on speech in Bulgaria, and their potential empowerment, even in another language, in Scotland. A drunken Svetan compares the silences he associates with Bulgarian with the freedoms he might aspire to in English:

> Nobody shouts in Bulgaria. Did you know that? We speak very quietly in the bars and cafés. My little girl, she's four, she goes to nursery. Ssssh! Got to be careful what you say. Kids talk to other kids, and other parents, and teachers. Who knows what side they're on?
>
> Well, now it's time to make a noise. . . .
>
> I'm sick of keeping quiet. Time to make a noise!

(I, x, p. 46)

In Scotland, culture has been celebrated as one of the key factors that made devolution possible. Both the economic success and the popular appeal of our artists bolstered a positive and outward-looking version of our culture. But a significant part of Scottish culture in the 1980s and even in the 1990s lay in contentment to be 'not English': for example, 'Scottish collective identity defines itself, to a significant degree, by differences in attitudes, values, and behaviour between the Scots and the English.'[16] Writing about devolution and television, Jane Sillars is right to describe 'a trend to explore differences *from* Scotland; while differences *within* Scotland have been put to one side'.[17] Part of the project of culture – and of criticism – in the post-devolution world is to recognize and analyze the variety and diversity of 'differences *within* Scotland', to reinvent identity as more that reactive, and much more than 'not English'.

Just as in *Further than the Furthest Thing*, *Shetland Saga* contrasts the potential flexibility of identities on the margins with the problems of nationhood and political idenity that is limited and constrained and fixed by economics. The play offers the potential for new hybrid identities through the negotiation of new connections and roles, through new relationships. While the sailors are debarred from returning to their original home, Glover's point of humanist optimism is that despite globalization, despite international capital and politics, people on the margins can make connections, and that identities can and do shift and adapt. She presents the potential for new smaller connections to be made and for new identities of be forged – and again, as in Harris's play, these are identities framed in terms of family and locality.

'Home'

It is certainly the case that one of the key communities, one of the key identities in Scottish drama, is that of the family. Nicola McCartney's *Home* uses the paradigm of family to think through ideas of belonging and identity. The play is set in Scotland, in a slightly dilapidated house in a small seaside town on the west coast. But the Scottish setting is, perhaps, of marginal significance – in a sense, the setting of Scotland only matters in the way that in *Further than the Furthest Thing* the setting is Tristan da

Gillian Kerr as Jen and Hope Ross as Kate in Nicola McCartney's *Home*. Photo: Keith Brame.

Cuhna. For both playwrights these places are imaginary spaces – on the one hand an isolated, edge-of-the-world island, on the other a small, familiar place, but again on the edge, on the coast.

McCartney's use of place and character, language and structure is far from naturalistic. She writes a richly layered, structurally and linguistically intricate play. Indeed, one might argue that the play's structuring principle is not acts and scenes and conventional narrative or thematic models of the theatre. Instead McCartney constructs her play as a mind-map, with scenes making a huge variety of connections that cross and re-cross, double and re-double, repeat themselves, lead to one set of ideas, and then loop back to different ideas, interpretations, and images. The resulting thematic and linguistic density of this organizing principle makes it difficult to isolate themes and motifs and images. But two key areas of concern do

present themselves: ideas of community, and of belonging; and the motif of 'the return of the native'.

McCartney describes a family of women. Kate and Annie are sisters, now middle-aged and living close to each other. Jo and Jen are Annie's grown up, twenty-something daughters – Jen a successful Edinburgh-based Euro-lawyer, Jo living at home and living with the communication disorder, Asperger's Syndrome. Over two days the two pairs of sisters argue and scold, revisit childhood haunts, and remember ancient events both significant and inconsequential. Their conversations demonstrate the minutiae of stuff – memories, habits, actions, linguistic ellipses, and verbal shorthands – that unite families. For example, memories surrounding the death of Kath and Annie's mother are no more significant in the collective memory or the linguistic world of the family than is a misremembered story of

385

where and when a watch was bought, or how, as small children, Jo and Jen broke a skylight.

The particular nature of Jo's condition draws attention to this odd amassing of detail and its lack of order and structure. Jo's condition manifests itself in a series of rituals and repetitive behaviours, of fixed paths to and from places, of rearranging the contents of cupboards alphabetically, of keeping and telling time, of using language in a closely remembered and literal manner. Jo's over-determined routines highlight and expose the repetition and the rituals that also shape family life and that represent the codes of belonging, the key to being a member of *this* family. The seeming chaos of stuff that links Annie, Kath, Jo, and Jen as a family also acts as a metaphor for the mess of ideas, images, histories, myths, beliefs, words, habits that mark our other identities – including, perhaps, national identities.

Different Kinds of 'Return'

The play also contrasts two returns: the return of Jen to the family home for the weekend; and, the remembered return of Kath, who had emigrated to the United States for many years before returning to Scotland. The first is an important return of the native in terms of character and narrative development. The arrival of Jen sparks the action of the play, but also asks us to consider the limits of this recurrent convention of the return. When Jo questions Jen's motivations she implicitly challenges the structural function of the return:

JO: You don't listen. You just ride in here on your white charger and fix everything.

JEN: I'm trying to help you.

JO: On your white charger. Leave it!

[...]

JO: You're on your white charger, you are.

(Nicola McCartney, *Home*, xiv, p. 78)[18]

This questioning from within the community unsettles the convention of the returning native. Further, it is not the returning Jen

who is alone in insisting on change, who questions tradition and custom. Instead, the characters who remained turn the demand for change back on her. It is Jo, the character who stayed, who McCartney uses as the significantly active force in challenging the orthodoxies of family and of family ritual, the orthodoxies of gender representation, and conventions of belonging:

JO: Are you getting married?

JEN: I think so. Yes, I think so.

JO: I don't want to be your bridesmaid. Is that okay?

JEN: That's okay. You would be terrible at it anyway.

JO: I would be terrible at it. I know.

(xiv, p. 81)

The second return is the remembered return of Kath. And again this allows McCartney to question the assumptions of the drama of return. Is the return of the native – no matter what the circumstances, no matter what the passage of time, no matter the nature of the reception – always a return 'home'? Kath recalls her own returns in a typically bare manner:

> My father died.
> I came home
> For the funeral
> And my mother said
> She was pleased
> To see me.
> I felt
> Visible. . . .
>
> My mother died.
> She died
> And I came home for the funeral. . . .
>
> I went back. . . .
>
> After all that time
> After
> Thirteen years
> In
> Chicago Illinois
> Boy
> I said
> We're going home.

(v, p. 23–5)

For this play the answer is that the place of return is indeed home – but that this is a place, an identity, that is far from fixed.

Mary McCusker as Annie and Kate Dickie as Jo in Nicola McCartney's *Home*. Photo: Keith Brame.

McCartney unsettles the idea of family, recreating it as flexible, reimagining it as a community that can shift and alter and evolve, and can then tell new and different stories.[19] Home, for McCartney in this play, is a place that evolves and changes as much as any other community or identity. And, I would suggest, this flexibility in the nature and the purpose of family is remarkably unfamiliar in Scottish drama.

Conclusion

In the essay quoted earlier, David Greig and David Harrower argued for a drama that challenged identity, myth, and representation. In this discussion I have limited my examples to drama written by women and premiered in Scotland in 2000, but even in this small sample one can see a cultural exploration that aspires to this project, that looks beyond Scotland and tests itself against other ideas, forms and narratives.

This dramaturgical experimentation has resulted in an innovative range of representations within Scottish theatre and has encouraged a reassessment of the environment, the milieu of Scottish drama. In this regard the plays of Nicola McCartney and Zinnie Harris mark a new and highly sophisticated engagement with the nature of writing in a small country – writing that is distinguished by a critical engagement with the representational conventions of that nation, as well as by an outward-looking and internationalist dynamic.

My paper has three underlying principles. Firstly, that devolution will shift how we create and imagine and represent Scotland. I would argue that theatre-makers working in Scotland – and my examples here have been the playwrights Harris, Glover, and McCartney – do aim to meet the challenges of a new cultural and political Scotland. And that they have done so by adopting a dramaturgy, by telling stories that are *both* international and outward-looking *and* essentially and immediately committed to work within and about Scottish society. And it is certainly the case that it is political devolution and the creation of the new Scottish parliament that insist that these dynamics can no longer be interpreted as mutually exclusive.

Secondly, I made the arguably self-evident point that identity remains a significant area of concern, that gender matters, and that feminist practice aims to promote new or alternative approaches to conventional representations. My examples of *Further than the Furthest Thing*, *Shetland Saga*, and *Home* aimed to show that. And thirdly I considered how, because of the orthodoxies of Scottish cultural practices and criticism, when challenging the conventions of narrative or of gender representation, artists also challenge the conventions of representing and responding to the nation. In the diversity of new Scottish plays we see artists challenge expectation, orthodoxy, and above all themselves.

In each of the plays I have mentioned women are placed at the very centre, and, through their characterization, their structural roles, their presence within the narrative, they offer alternative models to the orthodoxies of conventional Scottish culture. These challenges ask us to reconsider our understanding of and responses to Scotland and to Scottish culture. I would suggest that these plays demonstrate the very same interrogation of identity, of self, and indeed of nation that we need to apply to our new, post-devolution democracy.

My fourth and final point asks, 'Where next?' If we agree that devolution matters in terms of representation; if we agree that devolution might just impact on the type of art being made; if we agree that feminist art and criticism might unsettle representational and critical orthodoxies: then we should anticipate that devolution will result in shifts in the criticism of and for Scotland.

In a period of transition, creation, and re-creation within Scottish society, the demands on the nation's institutions and on our artists have never been more pressing: in this context Scottish criticism must also take on new responsibilities, and evolve and adapt to the new Scotland. Devolution must result in shifts in the criticism of and for Scotland.

At present, I don't know what that new criticism, that new critical rhetoric will be. I rather think it might be too early to be able to be clear on the 'Scottish solution' for contemporary criticism. But I think we should begin to look to contemporary art and artists to see if there are clues there. And perhaps reference to contemporary artists, analyzing their questioning of representational and narrative orthodoxies, will present new models that criticism can adapt and use.

The work of creative artists demonstrates a repertoire of questions, propositions, and reflections on the nature and the role of Scotland. Contemporary representation allows for versions of community that are flexible and fuzzy, that embrace identities that are evolutionary rather than fixed, and that tell stories that mix cultural specificity with bold internationalism. This diversity seems to offer a significant paradigm for the work of cultural criticisms in contemporary Scotland, where the demands on the cultural critic match the demands placed on the creative artist, as we are all challenged to participate in and contribute to a critical and reflective engagement with the art and the infrastructures, the representations and the identities of contemporary Scotland.[20]

Notes and References

1. Quotations are from Sue Glover, *Shetland Saga* (London: Nick Hern Books, 2000).

2. Benedict Anderson, *Imagined Communities: Reflections on the Origin and Rise of Nationalism* (London: Verso, 1990), p. 15.

3. See, for example, Cairns Craig, 'Myths against History: Tartanry and Kailyard in Nineteenth-Century Scottish Literature', in Colin McArthur, ed., *Scotch Reels: Scotland in Cinema and Television* (London: British Film Institute, 1982), p. 7–15; and David McCrone, *Understanding Scotland: the Sociology of a Stateless Nation* (London: Routledge, 1992).

4. These issues are raised in Craig Beveridge and Ronald Turnbull, *The Eclipse of Scottish Culture: Inferiorism and the Intellectuals* (Edinburgh: Polygon, 1989); and Tom Nairn, *The Break-Up of Britain: Crisis and Neo-Nationalism* (London: Verso, second ed., 1981).

5. The term 'fuzzy frontiers' is described by Robin Cohen, *Frontiers of Identity: the British and Others* (London: Longman, 1994).

6. McCrone, *Understanding Scotland*, p. 190.

7. See Cairns Craig, 'Myths against History', p. 7–15.

8. McCrone, 'Representing Scotland: Culture and Nationalism' in David McCrone, Stephen Kendrick and Pat Straw, ed., *The Making of Scotland: Nation, Culture, and Social Change* (Edinburgh: Edinburgh University Press, 1989), p. 172.

9. McCrone, 'Representing Scotland', p. 168, 172.

10. In passing, I would certainly consider that, in our post-devolution context, critics and practitioners alike might do well to interrogate and to reframe just what it is they want 'national' to mean. In a post-devolution context just what 'national' might actually mean is a key area of debate for critics and practitioners. A key indication of the new politics of Scotland is that a Labour/Liberal coalition government is prepared to be so sure about culture as a way of representing our *national* identity – when that national identity is assumed to be Scottish as opposed to British.

This is exciting because such confidence is a reflection of the diversity of representation that exists within contemporary Scottish culture. However, the positive aspect of confidence and investment in ideas and issues of national identity and representation also distracts attention from a critical flaw in the thinking and analysis that frames the key policy document, the statements and models of policy provision in Scotland at the moment. The Scottish Executive's *National Cultural Strategy* (2000) is less confident when examining infrastructure and the internal power structures for culture in Scotland. There are, for example, unresolved issues surrounding the role(s) of our existing national institutions – music, dance, opera, museums, and galleries – let alone the new ones such as the proposed Scottish Film Studios and Scottish National Theatre. It seems much easier to do more research into the pragmatics of what these organizations will look like, what they will cost, and what they might earn, rather than tackling the more difficult question of what, within the context of devolution, the role of a 'national' organization might be.

11. David Harrower and David Greig, 'Why a New Scotland Must Have a Properly-Funded Theatre', *The Scotsman*, 25 November 1997, p. 15.

12. Adrienne Scullion, 'Feminine Pleasures and Masculine Indignities: Gender and Community in Scottish Drama', in Christopher Whyte, ed., *Gendering the Nation: Studies in Modern Scottish Literature* (Edinburgh: Edinburgh University Press, 1995), p. 169–204.

13. I should like to preface my analysis with the following. When I presented a version of this paper as a lecture one member of the audience was quick to make a vehement interjection. Identifying himself as Zinnie Harris's husband, he strongly disagreed with my readings of *Further than the Furthest Thing* on the grounds that they were not, he claimed, what Harris had intended. He stated that I was wrong to see this play as in any sense Scottish and that it was not to be understood as a response to or part of contemporary Scottish culture. In particular he felt that it had no connection with the cultural project that Greig and Harrower's essay called for. He felt that the structure of my paper suggested that I was casting all three plays as direct responses to their newspaper article. I was surprised by this intervention on a number of levels, but should perhaps clarify one point. My project is not to create a new canon of Scottish plays or to offer silly or wilful or inappropriate definitions of the contemporary Scottish play. My critical purpose is rather more selfish and introspective than that: to analyze the experience of contemporary culture within Scotland in order to test and challenge and change its criticism.

14. Quotations are from Zinnie Harris, *Further than the Furthest Thing* (London: Faber and Faber, 2000).

15. See, for example, Sue Glover's *The Straw Chair* (Traverse/Focus, 1988) and *Bondagers* (Traverse, 1991). I have discussed this in my essays 'Feminine Pleasures and Masculine Indignities', p. 169–204; and 'Contemporary Scottish Women Playwrights', *The Cambridge Companion to Modern British Women Playwrights*, ed. Janelle Reinelt and Elaine Aston (Cambridge: Cambridge University Press, 2000), p. 94–118. See also Jan McDonald, 'Scottish Women Dramatists since 1945', *A History of Scottish Women's Writing*, ed. Douglas Gifford and Dorothy McMillan (Edinburgh: Edinburgh University Press, 1997), p. 494–513; and, Ksenija Horvat and Barbara Bell, 'Sue Glover, Rona Munro, Lara Jane Bunting: Echoes and Open Spaces', *Contemporary Scottish Women Writers*, ed. Aileen Christianson and Alison Lumsden (Edinburgh: Edinburgh University Press, 2000), p. 65–78.

16. Peter Meech and Richard Kilborn, 'Media and Identity in a Stateless Nation: the Case of Scotland', *Media, Culture and Society*, XIV, No. 2 (1992), p. 245–59, p. 246.

17. Jane Sillars, 'Drama, Devolution, and Dominant Representations', *The Media in Britain: Current Debates and Developments*, ed. Jane Stokes and Anna Reading (Basingstoke: Macmillan, 1999), p. 246–54, p. 252.

18. Quotations are from a typescript copy of the final version of the play.

19. This is an evolution of ideas McCartney explores in *Heritage* (Traverse, 1998). This is a play set in Saskatchewan and tells of the experiences of first, second, and even third generation Irish emigrants, and the clash of old and new identities. The play spans a period of six years from 1914 to 1920, describing the impact of events in Europe, both during the war and at the Easter Uprising. It is crucially concerned with the weight and meaning of Ireland, the nature and purpose of identity, and definitions of home. What is at stake in the play are, of course, definitions of Irishness, and what remains deliberately marginalized is the idea and nature of

Canadian identity. See Nicola McCartney, *Heritage* (Edinburgh: Traverse, 1998).

20. When I gave this paper as a lecture, I concluded with a rather personal point about the title of my presentation. I noted that my talk had not been about 'self and nation' at all – or at least it had not been about 'self and nation' in any abstract or objective way. Instead, I argued that what my talk had been about was '*my* self' and '*my* nation', and about taking the opportunity to think through my role as a critic, and, indeed, as a theatre scholar, within my new nation, and asking what role my work had in this context, and how I can use my discipline to participate in and contribute to a critical and reflective engagement with the art and the infra-structures of Scotland. These important questions will, I think, underlie much of the critical work produced in Scotland in the years to come.

Bibliography

Benedict Anderson, *Imagined Communities: Reflections on the Origin and Rise of Nationalism* (London: Verso, 1990).

Frank Bechhofer, David McCrone, Richard Kiely, and Robert Stewart, 'Constructing National Identities: Arts and Landed Elites in Scotland', *Sociology*, XXXIII, No. 3 (1999), p. 515–34.

Craig Beveridge and Ronald Turnbull, *Scotland after Enlightenment: Image and Tradition in Modern Scottish Culture* (Edinburgh: Polygon, 1997).

———, *The Eclipse of Scottish Culture: Inferiorism and the Intellectuals* (Edinburgh: Polygon, 1989).

Aileen Christianson and Alison Lumsden, ed., *Contemporary Scottish Women Writers* (Edinburgh: Edinburgh University Press, 2000).

Robin Cohen, *Frontiers of Identity: the British and Others* (London: Longman, 1994).

Clifford Geertz, 'The Integrative Revolution: Primordial Sentiments and Civil Politics in the New States', *Old Societies and New States: the Quest for Modernity in Asia and Africa*, ed. Geertz (New York: Free Press, 1963), p. 107–113.

Ernest Gellner, *Nations and Nationalism* (Oxford: Blackwell, 1983).

Sue Glover, *Shetland Saga* (London: Nick Hern, 2000).

———, *Bondagers* and *The Straw Chair* (London: Methuen, 1997).

Monserrat Guibernau, *Nations without States: Political Communities in a Global Age* (Cambridge: Polity Press, 1999).

Stuart Hall and Paul de Gay, ed., *Questions of Cultural Identity* (London: Sage, 1996).

Zinnie Harris, *Further than the Furthest Thing* (London: Faber and Faber, 2000).

David Harrower and David Greig, 'Why a New Scotland Must Have a Properly Funded Theatre', *The Scotsman* 25 November 1997, p. 15.

John Hutchinson and Anthony D. Smith, ed., *Nationalism* (Oxford: Oxford University Press, 2000).

Declan Kiberd, *Inventing Ireland: the Literature of the Modern Nation* (London: Vintage, 1996).

Colin McArthur, ed., *Scotch Reels: Scotland in Cinema and Television* (London: British Film Institute, 1982).

Nicola McCartney, *Home* (typescript, 2000).

———, *Heritage* (Edinburgh: Traverse, 1998).

David McCrone, *The Sociology of Nationalism* (London; New York: Routledge, 1998).

———, *Understanding Scotland: the Sociology of a Stateless Nation* (London; New York: Routledge, 1992).

David McCrone, Stephen Kendrick, and Pat Straw, ed., *The Making of Scotland: Nation, Culture and Social Change* (Edinburgh: Edinburgh University Press, 1989).

Jan McDonald, 'Scottish Women Dramatists since 1945', *A History of Scottish Women's Writing*, ed. Douglas Gifford and Dorothy McMillan (Edinburgh: Edinburgh University Press, 1997), p. 494–513.

Peter Meech and Richard Kilborn, 'Media and Identity in a Stateless Nation: the Case of Scotland', *Media, Culture and Society*, XIV, No. 2 (1992), p. 245–59.

Tom Nairn, *The Break-Up of Britain: Crisis and Neo-Nationalism* (London: Verso, second ed., 1981).

Murray G. H. Pittock, *Celtic Identity and the British Image* (Manchester; New York: Manchester University Press, 1999).

Adrienne Scullion, 'Contemporary Scottish Women Playwrights', *The Cambridge Companion to Modern British Women Playwrights*, ed. Janelle Reinelt and Elaine Aston (Cambridge: Cambridge University Press, 2000), p. 94–118.

———, 'Feminine Pleasures and Masculine Indignities: Gender and Community in Scottish Drama', *Gendering the Nation: Studies in Modern Scottish Literature*, ed. Christopher Whyte (Edinburgh: Edinburgh University Press, 1995), p. 169-204.

Jane Sillars, 'Drama, Devolution and Dominant Representations', *The Media in Britain: Current Debates and Developments*, ed. Jane Stokes and Anna Reading (Basingstoke: Macmillan, 1999), p. 246–54.

Anthony D Smith, *National Identity* (Harmondsworth: Penguin, 1991).

———, 'The Myth of the "Modern Nation" and the Myth of Nation', *Ethnic and Racial Studies*, I, No. 1 (1988), p. 1–26.

NTQ Reports and Announcements

Mary Brewer

Fierce! 2001

Report on the fourth international festival of cutting-edge European live art.

FIERCE, formerly Queerfest, is an annual international festival that premieres cutting-edge live art from Europe, the US, and Russia at a variety of venues across the Midlands. Running since 1998, it has been increasing in scope, profile, and prestige with every festival. Mark Ball, who has organized the festival since its inception, describes the aim of Fierce as presenting transgressive work that challenges sex-gender norms both in terms of its content and its form; and, while most of the work is by les/bi/gay-identified performers, Fierce is open to presenting any innovative and provocative live art about race/sex/gendered identities.

This year's programme of fourteen events kicked off with a launch party at Kudos in central Birmingham featuring 'white trash' queen Tina C. Besides the chance to sing along with Tina, Fierce offered the opportunity to catch *Double Agency*, latest work by the American duo Split Britches, Karim Karim's *Anywhere Anyone*, Raimund Hoghe's *Lettere Amorose*, Moti Roti's *Plain Magic*, and The Island Connection's *Come Midnight I'm Gone*. Also featured were the outrageous antics of Ursula Martinez in *Show Off*, La Ribot's exquisitely contemplative *Still Distinguished*, and Oleg Kulik's *Two Kuliks*, created especially for Fierce.

You could also see internationally acclaimed Franko B performing *Oh Lover Boy*, a stunning piece about images of painting which saw him lying on a raised metal bed bleeding onto a canvas below, and the controversial performance of lap-dancing lecturer Cathy MacGregor in *Scarlett's Story*. And spectators were given the chance to feed back their own opinions by taking part in a *Live Late Review* organized by the New Work Network at the Midlands Arts Centre.

However, Fierce is about more than simply bringing new national and international work to Midland audiences; its mission is also to stimulate the development of experimental live art in local communities across the region, firstly by making available innovative live art through the commissioning of theatre events. This year the festival sponsored *Oh Lover Boy*, *Two Kuliks*, and *D>Generate*, a collaboration between the Munich-based trio Chicks on Speed, the Birmingham-based musician Sand, and the visual artist Ravi Deepres.

Secondly, Fierce aims to facilitate the establishment of links and collaborative efforts among national and international performers and local artists. That the work showcased by Fierce has proved inspirational to local performers as well as audiences could be seen in the work of GAPP – Gay and Performing Proudly, a group of professional and non-professional gay performers. Their *Gay Adventures Past and Present* emerged out of Queerfest in 1999, under the direction of US performance artist Tim Miller.

A highlight of this year's festival was Ursula Martinez' *Show Off*. Featuring Martinez reflecting on the creation of the self in performance, this ranked high for sheer entertainment value and

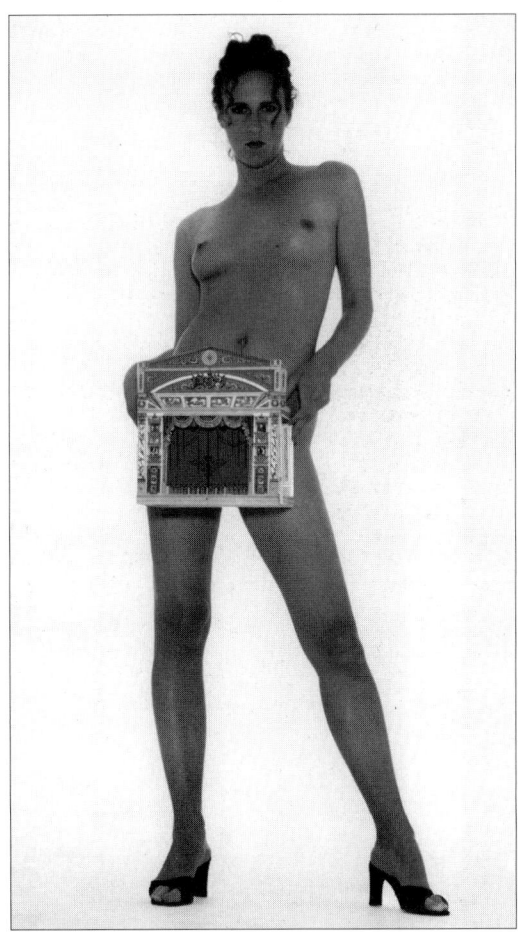

unadulterated fun while addressing some very complex postmodern ideas about the performativity of identity in a way that a general audience could understand and enjoy. A thought-provoking piece of political theatre, *Show Off* was all the more effective for its complete lack of didacticism.

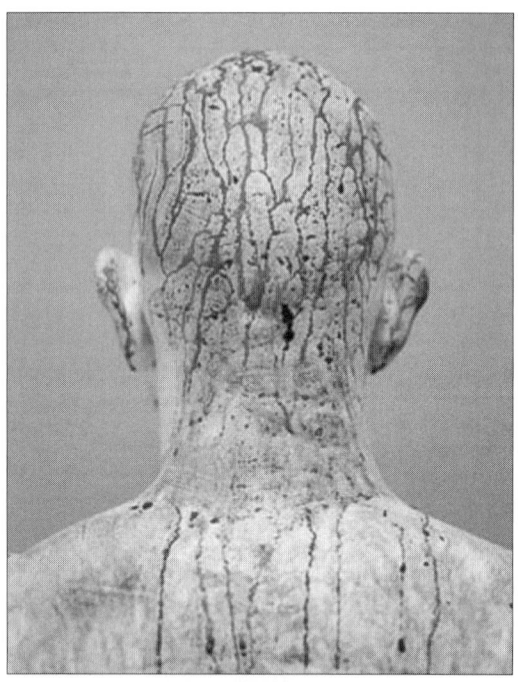

Opening with a flirtatious strip-tease routine, Martinez subverted the intrinsic banality of female stripping and its potential to render the female as sexual object by performing a series of remarkable and very humorous magic tricks with a napkin while she stripped (at one point pulling the napkin out of her vagina).

The parts where she engages in a dialogue *via* 'video-link' with her *other* self, a health and safety officer, and when the audience is invited to spot the actor as opposed to the 'real' person in a series of video clips, both demonstrated in a clear and amusing way the notion of being-as-playing. The several sketches that make up *Show Off* effectively challenge the idea that any form of identity, sexual or otherwise, is fixed or unitary; and to call into question the idea that normative constructions of gender and sexuality are themselves political fictions still represents an important political gesture for queer theatre.

A contrast to *Show Off* was *Scarlett's Story*, devised and performed by Cathy MacGregor, based on her experiences working as a dancer in a topless show bar. This certainly met Fierce's criteria for provocative fare, though sadly in this case by provoking the spectator's irritation. MacGregor's performance notes state that her personal exploration of the sex industry has enabled her to gain insights into how its reality conforms to the stereotypes surrounding dancers: 'Like all stereotypes, there were elements of truth in it but there was also a great more diversity and satisfaction in the experience than one might have been led to expect.'

Notwithstanding, it was difficult to see where and how MacGregor's representation of an erotic dancer rose above the level of stereotype. The piece offered scant evidence of any satisfaction, heightened feminist consciousness, or liberation (apart from one's overdraft perhaps) to be gained from working within the sex industry. If the message is that getting your kit off for money equates to female power, didn't we hear that from Madonna back in the 'eighties?

Scarlett's Story lacks the warmth, humour, and lightly ironic sense of Annie Sprinkle's *Postporn Modern*, for instance. Watching Sprinkle one gets the sense that here is a woman enjoying herself and celebrating her sexuality, whereas MacGregor appears to despise most elements of the trade, particularly the male punters. Despite positioning herself as a sex radical, she treats the audience to a catalogue of complaints about how hard the work is and how boring. Are we supposed to be surprised that MacGregor thinks about making a hot cup of tea while gyrating round a pole or that many of the male customers hold virulently degrading stereotypes of woman-as-whore? On the whole, this was a very ordinary piece of theatre, over-long and with far too much repetitive strip-dancing.

Still Distinguished by La Ribot and Kulik's *Two Kuliks* give a sense of the diversity of performance presented at Fierce. *Still Distinguished* comprises eight distinct performance pieces and forms part of a larger project, *Piezas Distinguidas*, begun in 1993. So far, thirty-four performances have been created, with the aim of eventually producing one hundred different pieces. Here, the event benefited from its setting in the foyer of the New Art Gallery, Walsall, where the highly appreciative and mainly local audience followed the nude La Ribot around an open playing space littered with props and surrounded by video stills and sound speakers.

Still Distinguished offered a multi-media feast for the senses that was paradoxically mesmerizing in its stillness and control. In the last two pieces, *Zurratada* and *S Liquide*, one watched La Ribot drinking a bottle of water while sinking slowly to the floor, and then we listened to her breathing as she lay in a fetal posture, her body wrapped in gold foil. In these pieces and others, La Ribot stripped the category of the sexual, the human, down to its most elemental functions, while at the same time elevating such simple acts as breathing, drinking, and desiring into an elegant art form that was beautiful to watch. The work was intentionally elusive in meaning, refusing categorization, and all the more exciting for doing so. More than any other piece in the festival, this left me thinking long after the performance had ended.

Opposite page: top: Franko B performing in *Oh Lover Boy*; below: Oleg Kulik's *Two Kuliks*, created especially for Fierce. This page, above: GAPP (Gay and Performing Proudly) in *Gay Adventures Past and Present*; below: *Double Agency*, latest work by the American duo Split Britches.

Kulik's performance was also expertly located in an upper room at Birmingham's Ikon Gallery. The cathedral-like archways of the room combined with the cool blue lighting and the dais on which Kulik performed, gave the piece an aura of ancient ritual that harmonized nicely with its theme, since the performance represented a dialogue between the conscious and unconscious self. Entering the space to traditional Russian music, Kulik, after undressing, and with a paintbrush strapped to his forehead, applies red paint to the contours of his facial image as it is projected onto a large piece of glass. Meanwhile, behind him, three images of his face were projected onto an elevated screen, each of which could be seen reacting with puzzled, angry, or sometimes tortured expressions to his brushstrokes.

The act of painting symbolizes Kulik's attempt to master his fears – the continuous unconscious narrative that tells him he is 'bullshit' or 'not an artist'. The impossibility of ever gaining complete mastery over our personal demons and all the accompanying emotional frustration and disappointment are amplified when Kulik ends the performance by shattering the glass with a violent head-butt. That we all are vulnerable to playing this kind of psychological game with ourselves, in which we attempt to master our alter-ego by fashioning counter-narratives, allows this work a wide scope for collective resonance with an audience. Though brief, roughly twenty minutes, this was a brave, raw, and forceful piece of theatre, risky for the way the performer was willing to expose himself psychically as much as physically, and compelling by virtue of Kulik's ability to establish a visceral bond with his audience, a connection that sparks reflection about how one negotiates one's own internal dialogues.

Karim Karim's three performance pieces – *Anywhere Anyone*, *Murphy's Law*, and *Exhausted* – gave Fierce its multi-cultural flavour. *Anywhere Anyone* is an extended solo dance piece to a blend of musical styles that focuses on notions of cultural hybridity – the intersection of gender, sexual, racial, and cultural difference. The work emerges out of the performer's own life, Karim having been born in Uganda, raised in Canada, and educated in the US, before going to live and work in Spain. Karim describes *Anywhere Anyone* as 'a nomadic story' for the way that 'it crosses the divisions of race and culture, not fusing them, but layering and combining them, the way we re-identify ourselves after time in a new land'. Across a stage space divided by different coloured painted lines and ethnic costume, Karim charts his search for home-place – a space where he can locate himself and that will enable him successfully to resist the dominant forces which would reduce him to any one of his possible identities.

Exhausted (performed with Susan Kempster), deals with a search for balance, and is infused with Beckettian overtones. Through a combination of dance and mime, Karim and Kempster explore the theme of alienation, the difficulty of establishing psychic equilibrium within the context of the frenetic pace of urban life in late capitalist democracies, and the futility of the struggle against life-forces, ageing, and eventual death. Although this work fitted least well within the larger thematic framework of Fierce, it was a rewarding theatrical experience which unfortunately did not attract the audience it deserved.

However, the overall success of the festival, in terms of attendance figures, critical notice, and publicly funded as well as commercial sponsorship, suggests that there is a significant audience beyond London, both queer and straight, for radical work challenging issues of representation of les/bi/gay communities. In fact, of those attending Fierce 2001, some 70 per cent identified as straight and 30 per cent as gay or lesbian. Thus Fierce is helping to resist the marginalization of queer performers – effectively bringing queer work into the mainstream without mainstreaming it.

Moreover, at a time when theatre attendance is declining, particularly among younger spectators, it is further encouraging to learn that Fierce has developed a loyal audience of under-thirties who would not normally choose theatre as a form of entertainment. The ability to attract a young audience is due not only to the 'hip' content of the live art itself but, equally important, to the fact that much of the work gets staged in non-traditional venues such as bars, clubs, and galleries, where people who might not be comfortable in a traditional theatre space feel more at their ease. Another contributory factor is the commitment of the festival's organizers to keeping ticket prices low, in order to make the events accessible to as wide a local audience as possible.

When asked what makes Fierce unique as a theatre festival, Mark Ball identified its emphasis on fostering a sense of ownership across a range of people in the region – performers, professional and amateur, queer and ethnic communities, venue managers, and sponsors. As to how Fierce may develop in future, Ball wants to increase partner links with local communities, and especially galleries, clubs, and businesses so that more work may be shown in non-traditional spaces. He would also like to enhance the festival's impact on theatre in the Midlands through continuing to bring new live art to the area, and, more important, by sponsoring new work involving local artists, as well as through supporting workshops and local training programmes. The principal aim of Fierce in the next five years will thus be to operate as a collective project across a range of communities in the Midlands.

Fierce 2002 will take place in May. For further information on next year's festival you can e-mail fierce@fierceearth.com or ring 0121-244-8080.

NTQ Book Reviews

edited by Bella Merlin

Mary Bly
**Queer Virgins and Virgin Queans on
the Early Modern Stage**
Oxford University Press, 2000. 213 p. £35.00
ISBN: 0-19-818699-1.

I have often wondered whether boy actors were erotic objects when they were dressed as males as well as when they were dressed as females. I think I have found my answer in Mary Bly's account of the first Whitefriars theatre. This theatre and company are not widely known. It was a short-lived venture, operating for about a year from spring 1607, and its playwrights tended to be amateurs who produced very little. At the same time, these playwrights also ran the theatre – and, according to Bly's argument, they pitched their work at a very specific audience. That audience, gathering in a seedy area of London, were a literary coterie who could pick up on allusions and borrowings between texts. They also enjoyed homoerotic jokes. And it is these jokes – or, to be more precise, this flood of obscene puns – which constitute Bly's main vehicle into the material.

She does some very detailed close-up reading to show how the puns characteristically work. This method may be word-based, but it is not narrowly literary: Bly is interested in how words construct gendered identities. And her account of current thinking about early-modern gender and sexuality in its fullness and readability is very student-friendly. So, having trained the reader of her book to be an early seventeenth-century spectator, she then traces relationships between the plays and the texts they borrow from, and then steps back again to explore the relations between people connected with the theatre. This process brings into view a homoerotic culture. Which is where I found my answer.

SIMON SHEPHERD

Kenneth Borris
**Allegory and Epic in English Renaissance
Literature: Heroic Form in Sidney, Spenser,
and Milton**
Cambridge University Press, 2000. 320 p. £40.00.
ISBN: 0-521-78129-9.

Renaissance allegory has been associated with the end of medievalism, but in this book Borris contends that the mode was substantially influenced by new access to classical texts which 'changed and revitalized literary conceptions' about it. Other factors such as the Reformation, the Council of Trent, and the Counter Reformation, 'reinforced the contemporary topicality of utilitarian or morally instrumental approaches to literature, and thus of allegorism itself'.

In the early modern period, heroic poetry by Homer and Virgil was considered especially important, and, in the sixteenth-century accounts of literary genres, epic and allegory were closely connected. Sidney's *Arcadia*, Spenser's *Faerie Queene*, and Milton's *Paradise Lost* here receive fresh readings to confront previous critical interpretations which assumed that allegory became less important after 1600. Borris emphasizes the allegorical nature of Sidney's writing and positions him as Spenser's immediate literary progenitor. He also contends that, contrary to recent critical opinion, Spenser did not abandon allegory in the later books of *The Faerie Queene* and shows that episodes dismissed as allegorically simple, such as the one featuring Arthur, Turpine, Enias and the Savage in Book 6, are complex: Enias evokes the classical hero Aeneas, the figure of Judas Iscariot, and even Jesus Christ.

Spenser's presentation of Christian virtues anticipates Milton's *Paradise Lost*, although Milton's epic (whose allegory is critically under-examined) does not celebrate the nation as Spenser's does. In the final three chapters of this book, Borris relates the Christian motif of the doctrine of the mystical church to that of composite heroism from allegorical epic, and explains that heroism in Milton's poem is Christ-centred. Sidney, Spenser, and Milton used allegory differently but shared an interest in the mode's capacity for psychological subtlety, and therefore Borris's argument will interest students of the epic as well as those concerned with theatrical devices.

JOAN FITZPATRICK

Catherine Burroughs, ed.
**Women in British Romantic Theatre:
Drama, Performance, and Society, 1790–1840**
Cambridge University Press, 2000. xvi, 344 p.
£37.50.
ISBN: 0-521-66224-9.

This is a good time to be interested in women theatre practitioners who worked in Britain and America in the late eighteenth and nineteenth centuries. Over the past four or five years, several ground-breaking monographs and a raft of exhilarating collections and essays have been published. This work has expanded the locus of study very significantly. It has unearthed 'new' plays and playwrights. It has reset interpretations of plays already reasonably well known. It has presented challenging methodological and historiographical debates. Catherine Burroughs – along with scholars such as Ellen Donkin, Tracy Davis, Jacky Bratton, Susan Bennet, Julie Carlson, and Jeffrey Cox – has been at the centre of this work, which is now further strengthened in a collection which focuses attention on the Romantic period, and on the women dramatists and performers working in the fifty years following the French Revolution.

The volume consists of eleven new essays organized into five areas of thematic concern: 'Historical Contexts: Revolution and Entrenchment', 'Nations, Households, Dramaturgy', 'Performance and Closet Drama', 'Criticism and Theory', and 'Translation, Adaptation, Revision'. Analysis and interpretation of the careers and work of Joanna Baillie, Sarah Siddons, and Elizabeth Inchbald thread through the entire collection and act as touchstones for testing and assessing other, lesser known practitioners such as Hannah More, Anne Yearsley, Anne Plumptre, and Jane Scott. The effect is of a complex, multi-layered theatre culture that achieves distinctive negotiations, both subtle and bold, across criticism and practice, text and performance, closet dramas and stage productions.

A particular feature of this volume is its interrogation of period criticism. Greg Kucich's essay highlights the 'split between effusive welcome and vigorous resistance' that marks contemporary reviews by male critics of the work of women playwrights. He underlines the bold countercultural potential of the contemporary woman playwright as he comments on the layers of patriarchal censorship and censure that she had to face. This work is paralleled by Marvin Carlson, who considers Inchbald's role as a critic in her series of biographical and critical prefaces for the twenty-five volume *British Drama* series in which, of course, 'she presumed to write critical commentary not only upon her own writings, but on those of other living dramatists, primarily men'.

Elsewhere debates around identity – and in particular national identity – allow Katherine Newey and Jeanne Moskal to elucidate the political subtexts of work by Baillie, Inchbald, Susanna Rowson, Hannah Cowley, Maria Edgeworth, and Mariana Starke. The appeal of the popular stage and of the wicked potential of melodrama is revealed in a reflection on a workshop-based investigation of Jane Scott's Romantic melodrama *Camilla the Amazon* (1817) by Jacky Bratton, Gilli Bush-Bailey, and a group of creative and committed undergraduates. Together they produce an account that is distinguished by its fun and its energy, as well as its dramaturgical and historical rigour. Burrough's collection is concerned with both literary and theatrical contexts and approaches and amply demonstrates the 'sharing of intellectual tools and practices from different disciplines' that characterizes work in this area.

ADRIENNE SCULLION

Bill Marshall and Robynn Stilwell, ed.
Musicals: Hollywood and Beyond
Exeter: Intellect Books, 2000. £14.95.
ISBN: 1-84150-003-8.

The film musical remains under-researched, and any academic attempt to rectify that is welcome, particularly so when, as promised and delivered here, the material ranges far beyond Hollywood, the power of whose lens (one might argue) has been directly proportional to the myopia of its owners. This is not just another book on the American film musical, but includes Spain (José Arroyo on *Las cosas del querer*), Germany (Tim Bergfelder on the 'Heimat' films and after, and Horst Claus and Anne Jäckel on *Der Kongress tanzt*), France (Sylvie Lindeperg and Bill Marshall on *Les Parapluies de Cherbourg*), Belgium (Cathy Fowler on *Golden Eighties*), and Greece (Lydia Papadimitriou on Hellenic and Romeic musicals). One cheer for this, though we need something on the communist musical, more on England than an anodyne study of Jarman, and something on Latin America, not to mention places further east, south, or north than these.

Within these terms, overwhelmingly those of Film Studies (sociology, cultural and subcultural history, and literature), there are some engaging and informative if modestly short essays. These include a reprint of Richard Dyer's classic on 'The Colour of Entertainment' and studies of Audrey Hepburn, Julie Andrews, Woody Allen, and the Marx Brothers, though 'zero patience' summed up my own reaction to Monica Pearl's piece on the film of that title. But the editors and the contributors never tell us what is a musical and what isn't, where to draw lines and create taxonomies, and how to examine and understand music in ways which make sense across a defined terrain.

They are also lazy and grudging with material, statistics, and presentation: we never get so much as a complete list of the musical numbers in a film and the blurb's claim to be initiating 'a new critical debate by approaching classic Hollywood films from perspectives such as "musicology"' is a nonsense. There is nothing in this book for the music student. Nor is there anything in it for the theatre student, musical theatre being ignored at every turn – as if *Show Boat* and the Rodgers and Hammerstein creations hadn't originated there! As far as I could detect, only once in this book has a contributor bothered to consult an unpublished primary source of any kind (even interviews). As I said, the film musical remains under-researched.

STEPHEN BANFIELD

Steven R. Centola, ed.
Arthur Miller: Echoes Down the Corridor
(Collected Essays 1944–2000)
London: Methuen, 2000. xviii, 332 p. £15.00 (hbk),
£9.99 (pbk).
ISBN: 0-413-75690-4 (hbk), 0-413-75680-7 (pbk).

This collection begins with a preface by the author himself, which remarks on its unexpected political orientation: Miller was surprised to see that the thrust of his work should so closely map onto public paradigm shifts. An introduction by the editor, Steven R. Centola, contextualizes the essays further, noting that the title comes from a line in Miller's play *The Crucible*, and indicates the way in which the essays 'echo' ideas both in the theatre and outside it.

The collection is arranged for the most part chronologically (the exceptions being the first two autobiographical essays and the final essays), and this format allows for connections across the diverse disciplines on which Miller writes. Indeed, a few of the essays refer back to each other, prompting connections which the reader may or may not have made independently. Centola argues that Miller is best examined as 'a chronicler of the historical procession of the twentieth century', and this is an apt assessment of Miller's collected work. Only a few of the essays are actually based on theatre or theatre criticism; most are historically or politically oriented, ranging across topics as diverse as juvenile delinquency, the Nazi war trials, and Clinton's affair with Monica Lewinsky (the public laundering of which Miller links to the Salem witch trials).

Of the essays on theatre, the reader finds Miller encountering Tennessee Williams, Ibsen, and himself. Essays that stand out particularly are the extract from '*Salesman* in Beijing', 'History and *The Crucible*', and '*Salesman* at Fifty'. The final essay, 'Subsidized Theatre', argues passionately that there will be no future in American theatre – and certainly no audience of young people – unless a subsidy system is introduced. As a companion text for Miller's dramatic work, this collection is far-ranging, illuminating, and at times comic. It should be of interest to any student or scholar of American theatre.

HEIDI SLETTEDAHL MACPHERSON

George Plimpton
The Playwrights at Work:
the 'Paris Review' Interviews
Harvill, 2000. 411 p. £12.00.
ISBN: 1-86046-783-0.

This third volume of the *Paris Review* 'Writers at Work' series features some of the big names of twentieth-century theatre. Although nowadays the journalistic interview is usually motivated by the desire to publicize the playwright's latest show, here the purpose is to explore the writer's work more deeply. Starting with Thornton Wilder and Lillian Hellman, the book includes Tennessee Williams, Arthur Miller, Neil Simon, Edward Albee, John Guare, Sam Shepard, and David Mamet. Such great white America males are joined by one black writer (August Wilson) and one continental (Eugene Ionesco). Encounters with Samuel Beckett, who refused to be interviewed, are revealingly described by Lawrence Shainberg, who met him during the 1980s. The interviewers, including Christopher Bigsby (Miller) and Susha Guppy (Stoppard), remain mercifully unintrusive.

In his introduction, John Lahr rightly emphasizes the importance of performance for the playwright, pointing out that 'the novelist never sees the reader walk out' on his work, and also quoting Guare's: 'You must keep people happy backstage because that affects what's onstage.' The different working methods of the writers are contrasted – from Williams's eight-hour-a-day autobiographical craftsmanship to Pinter's reliance on subconscious inspiration – and anecdotes abound. At one premiere, we watch Hellman getting drunk and vomiting; at another, Ionesco's dadaist entourage arrives, each member wearing a 'large turd' on their lapels.

The interviews (conducted between 1956 and 1999) vary in tone, with Wilder's patrician coolness and Miller's sincere didacticism giving way to Simon's loquacious jokiness and Mamet's combative precision. Most writers agree that plays originate with a silent image or chance phrase, most resort to metaphors to describe their working methods, and most are generous about their influences: usually Beckett, Pinter, and Brecht. All despise critics, if for different reasons. But, although useful as a source of speculation about the notoriously thorny relationship between autobiography and art, this collection also supports the idea that playwrights are superstitious, fragile, and unpredictable. It also suggests that, in Lahr's words, theatre 'is the last bastion of the individual voice'.

ALEKS SIERZ

Guillermo Gómez-Peña
Dangerous Border Crossers
London; New York: Routledge. 285 p. £14.99.
ISBN: 0-415-18237-9.

Of all the Latino theatre artists currently working in the USA, Guillermo Gómez-Peña is probably the most conspicuously known, at least in the British academic community. Whilst John Leguizamo's provocative solo performances have failed to resonate across these shores and Latino dramatists such as Maria Irene Fornes, Nilo Cruz, and

Caridad Svich remain largely unknown figures, Gómez-Peña has, through valuable associations with the Centre for Performance Research, become the touchstone for Latino performance studies. For those familiar with his polemical writings and performances, *Dangerous Border Crossers: the Artist Talks Back* develops terrain affectingly mapped out in earlier articles and interviews. Incorporating diary fragments, conversations with collaborators and critics, reworkings of earlier articles and essays, and selections of performance scripts, this is an ambitious and elegantly produced collage-volume.

As with other recent Routledge publications – Matthew Goulish's inspiring *39 Microlectures* and Tim Etchell's eloquent *Certain Fragments* come particularly to mind here – this is a volume which rewards those who are willing to dip into its rich pickings. The scope of the contributions is wide, and as befits an artist who seeks to distance himself from the confessional tone of diaries and autobiographies, the emphasis remains resolutely on the intersections between the political, social, and cultural as negotiated by a particular Mexican-American artist working in very particular contexts which are astutely delineated and theorized.

Categories are constantly and consistently re-thought. Romanticization is consciously avoided as Gómez-Peña charts artistic journeys mapped out against the larger picture of a nomadic life spent negotiating both geographical and political borders. Lavishly illustrated and imaginatively compiled, *Dangerous Border Crossers* is a thought-provoking reflection on the creation and consumption of art in rapidly changing times which wears its critical sophistication with refreshing lightness.

MARIA M. DELGADO

David Krasner, ed.
Method Acting Reconsidered
Hampshire: Macmillan, 2000. 312 p. £12.95.
ISBN: 0-333-91547-X

The premise behind this book is worthy: the desire to take far into the academic forum a discussion of the controversial Method schools of acting. The editor, David Krasner, has assembled twenty contributors from the realms of practical acting, directing, writing, and academic analysis and research, as well as accommodating those who are seeking to perpetuate or renegotiate the vocabulary of acting through drama schools and universities.

The book divides into four clear sections – Practice, Theory, Future, and Method Schools (this last being a small section constituting more of an appendix to the academic debate than a chapter in its own right). Krasner's extended introductory chapter throws up some very provo-cative ideas, including the juxtaposition of post-modern determinism with the desire for free will and its impact on twenty-first century acting practice. However, much of the book falls into the (perhaps unavoidable) trap facing practitioners who theorize and academics who expound practical systems.

The result is that in many ways the first two sections – Practice and Theory – are somewhat inflammatory. Although Krasner's introduction promises the alignment of American Method (be it Strasberg, Meisner, or Adler, between whose systems the book is keen to differentiate) with Stanislavsky's 'system', time and again the defence of one against the other leads to misinterpretation. Many ideas presented as new and illuminating are nothing more than Stanislavsky's own psycho-physical ideas (to be traced back as far as *An Actor Prepares*) attributed to the West rather than the East.

There are undoubtedly some fascinating ideas. Marc Gordon's analysis of Vakhtangov's influence, Deb Margolin's wonderfully written and meta-phoric synthesis of theory and practice, and Jean Dobie Giebel's chapter on Significant Action are particularly tasty. However, the latter's chapter suffers, along with David Wiles's 'Burden of Representation', in simply being too short. Just at the point when the intricate debate begins, the chapters end. By the time the third section (Future) is reached, however, the picture changes. In general, all writers in the third section seem more comfortable with juxtaposing theory and practice, added to which they have been provided with higher wordage, enabling more penetrative discussion. Here, Rhonda Blair and Paul Kassel both raise some fascinating and provocative issues, as well as bringing Stanislavsky more clearly into the picture.

Possibly the most rewarding chapter is the last serious contribution to the book. Dennis Beck's 'Paradox of the Method Actor' takes a pertinent and lucidly fresh look at Stanislavsky's 'dual consciousness' and the interaction between actor, character, and person. Furthermore, he reminds us that perhaps a real reconsideration of the Method and the 'system' needs a return to Eastern Europe.

BELLA MERLIN

Russell Jackson, ed.
The Cambridge Companion to Shakespeare on Film
Cambridge University Press, 2000. 342 p.
£13.95 (pbk), £37.50 (hbk).
ISBN 0 521-63975-1 (pbk), 0-521-63023-1 (hbk).

In the late 1930s, Graham Greene was moved to confess that he was 'less than ever convinced that there is an aesthetic justification for filming Shakespeare at all'. Some sixty years later, cinematic Shakespeare is more popular than at any time since the advent of sound, but, as this collection of essays shows, the debate as to Shakespeare's cinematic worthiness, and how to assess it, rages just as fiercely.

This comprehensively edited volume is divided into four parts, based on Adaptation, Genre, Directors, and Critical Issues. However, there is considerable overlap in all sections except the third, and – as Harry Keyishian's essay in Part One, 'Shakespeare and Movie Genre', shows – there is often an unresolved tension concerning whether the mode of analysis is cinematic or literary. Consequently, the criticism tends to approach film as interpretation of text rather than as a translation of material from one radically different art form to another. There are exceptions: Barbara Freedman's acute and elegant essay, 'Critical Junctures in Shakespeare's Screen History', probes this difference perceptively, while Carol Chillington Rutter's witty 'Looking at Shakespeare's Women' on film reverses the accepted procedure and uses film theory to look at Shakespeare's texts.

Elsewhere, Tony Howard is both concise and full of surprises in tackling a near impossible task in 'Shakespeare's Cinematic Offshoots' – giving overdue mention in the process to the long-neglected Shakespearean influences in the work of Michael Powell. Pamela Mason and Mark Sokolyansky contribute balanced and insightful accounts of the Shakespearean work of Orson Welles and Grigori Kozintsev respectively, and Neil Taylor discusses clearly and sensibly 'National and Racial Stereotypes in Shakespeare's Films'. Russell Jackson's own contributions reflect his dual incarnations as academic and as 'text advisor' on the films of Kenneth Branagh, and are characteristically witty and informative. Finally, this collection is an important addition to the 'Cambridge Companion' series, and one that prompts us to say, with the editor, 'You didn't think Shakespeare could be like this, did you?'

JONATHAN HOLMES

Christopher Innes, ed.
A Sourcebook on Naturalistic Theatre
Toronto: Routledge, 2000. 261 p.
ISBN: 0-415-15228-3 (hbk), 0-415-15229-1 (pbk).

Innes's sourcebook is invaluable, particularly for students of naturalist theatre and their tutors. A lucidly written first chapter places the movement with absolute scholarly precision in its various socio-political and theatrical contexts. Innes presents the terms 'naturalism' and 'realism' in all their glorious ambiguity, then proceeds to guide the reader up a precarious cliff-face of contrasting definitions. In this way, he demonstrates how their consistent usage – even in standard reference works discussing the specific literary and theatrical movement in question – is rare.

A logical solution is gently suggested – precisely the sort that drama undergraduates everywhere are thirsting for: why not (without absolutely denying the 'subtle distinction' between the two words) use 'Naturalism' with reference to the theoretical basis shared by relevant dramatists and 'Realism' to their intended effect and corresponding stage techniques? From this perspective, the same play can be considered as naturalistic *and* realistic. Indeed, Innes consistently gives equal attention to both theory and stage practice. Amongst his sources are political tracts, historical documents, theatre reviews, letters, practitioners' writings, photographs, and extracts from promptscripts. What is particularly admirable about the way in which Innes presents and draws together these sources is the fact that, in being selective, he ultimately rejects a reductionist approach and manages to express the breadth of the movement.

His choice of playwrights for the later, major chapters – Ibsen's *A Doll's House* and *Hedda Gabler*, Chekhov's *The Cherry Orchard* and *The Seagull*, and Shaw's *Mrs Warren's Profession* and *Heartbreak House* – is to some extent unconventional. However, as Innes rightly argues, Shaw was indirectly involved in the naturalist movement. Ruling out his work can only serve to distort our understanding. Conversely, Shaw's inclusion in the argument forces us to reconsider important qualities in the relevant plays of Ibsen and Chekhov that are not 'naturalistic'. Innes shatters the lens of strict naturalistic theory, and invites us to scrutinize the canon with a refreshing boldness. Packed full of information, this is a digestible and satisfying book, which points the way towards further research.

TERESA MURJAS

Kimberley W. Benston
Performing Blackness: Enactments of African-American Modernism
London; New York: Routledge, 2000. 386 p.
£16.99 (pbk), £50.00 (hbk).
ISBN: 0-415-00949-9 (pbk), 0-415-00948-0 (hbk).

This book offers a comprehensive, interdisciplinary evaluation of the relation between blackness and performance in African-American culture since the Black Arts Movement of the 1960s. *Performing Blackness* addresses the way in which African-American writers and performers have endeavoured to define black identity through a range of performance practices, including drama, poetry, music, and the modern-chant sermon. Benston reads theoretical and performance texts for each piece's particular sign and vision of blackness in relation to being and performance. Her interpretation of the work of Adrienne Kennedy and of

Ntozake Shange as constitutive elements within a Black Arts Movement (rather than as antithetical) affords new insights into our critical understanding of those artists' significant body of work. The discussions of Amiri Baraka's performative poetics and of the jazz of John Coltrane, which focus on the artists' respective resistance to conventional dramatic and musical narratives, are noteworthy for highlighting how their specific theatrical/musical forms represent political struggle through creative practice. The final chapter offers a critically revealing account of the relation of African-American autocritography, a genre which blends interpretive and autobiographical forms, to identity politics. The book also has useful appendices containing a selection of poems about Coltrane and sermon transcripts.

Performing Blackness offers some convincing evidence of the power of black performance to enable the black spectator not merely to recognize but to participate in determining a communal notion of black identity and to enable political solidarity. At the same time, its theoretically subtle appreciation of the complexity of modern black identity ensures that we do not lose sight of its provisionality. Its need for the reader to be thoroughly grounded in contemporary poststructuralist theory and postmodern debates about identity, combined with the theoretical density of its prose, make it inappropriate for all but the most advanced undergraduate readers. However, the book will prove valuable for researchers and postgraduate students working in the fields of drama and performance, cultural and race studies.

MARY BREWER

Nick Kaye
Site-Specific Art:
Performance, Place, and Documentation
London; New York: Routledge, 2000. 238 p.
£16.99.
ISBN: 0-415-18559-9.

This book represents an important and timely contribution to the field of site-specific art and performance. It is structured around sections on spaces, sites, material, and frames, providing not only a detailed and rigorous interrogation of the parameters of site-specific performance work, but also an accessible and thorough survey of the work of key practitioners in this field. The work is contextualized historically, and is used to illuminate the theoretical proposals that go to drive this study.

A detailed and thorough introduction opens and broadens definitions of site-specificity into a series of subtle negotiations between place and its production, the operation of language and readership, and the inherent stability of 'space as a practised place'. This observation, drawn from the work of Michel de Certeau, is developed by Kaye into a treatment of site-specific work as a point at which tensions – between site and work, between space and performance, between performance and visual arts/architecture – are staged. Thus the book itself, rather than seeking to codify site-specific practice, traverses a broad and diverse range of work.

The documentations, which Kaye describes as 'intervening' in the critical narrative, all deal differently with the challenge of documenting, for the page, work which is rooted in its site, its moment, and its place. This is perhaps one of the most interesting facets of the book – it is in itself a site-specific staging of its own (and the field's) central problem: the intersection of analysis and performance text. For this, and its many other good qualities, the book will be of key importance to students, scholars, and practitioners in its field, as well as containing much of interest to those engaged with architecture, visual arts, and performance.

SOPHIE NIELD

Richard Stone
You Should Have Been in Last Night
Lewes, 2000. £16.95.
ISBN: 1-85776-555-9.

Theatre people communicate their experiences through anecdotes, and in many ways anecdotes are what holds the profession together as a community. Pros meet and the stories flow. Exchanging stories about third parties is how you locate yourself in the theatre profession. Richard Stone was for many years a leading agent and producer, and the range of his activities has enabled him to assemble a good collection of anecdotes and publish them in a book, all proceeds going to Denville Hall and Brinsworth, retirement homes for actors and artistes. Unfortunately, he did not live long enough to enjoy a pleasure that would have redoubled when colleagues came up with answering stories to the ones in the book, as he died close to the publication date. With numerous stories, not the least of which refer to my local summer seasons in Saltburn where Stone met his future wife, the book has interesting revelations about how theatre agents and producers used to work in his time. Added to which, the proceeds from this book go to an excellent cause, so who can possibly resist it?

CLIVE BARKER